To Eli,
My Apologist in Training

To Christine

The stronger of the two strands
that when combined with God's make up a cord
that is not easily broken

Ecclesiastes 4-12

***

To Jeff McConnell and Rick Booye

Who helped me more than they might know

***

To Kyle McCulloch and Steven Bloyed

Who remind me everyday about the wonders of being

young at heart

***

And to my Mom

Who belongs in the hall of fame for caring people

Seeking God in a Twisting America

by

Robert Segotta

A quick look into our lethargic and apathetic attitudes toward God

A glance at American culture and how it is currently under assault

The derailment of Eastern thought and their latest bestseller

Differing world views and the religions at the forefront

The layman's interpretation of Christianity

The youthful perspective on God

The communication breakdown

Warning!
This is a guide to inspire curiosity. All conclusions contained on the
following pages are to be carefully examined and scrutinized.

authorHOUSE®

AuthorHouse™
1663 Liberty Drive
Bloomington, IN 47403
www.authorhouse.com
Phone: 1-800-839-8640

First published by AuthorHouse 10/16/2009

ISBN: 978-1-4490-3667-6 (e)
ISBN: 978-1-4490-3669-0 (sc)
ISBN: 978-1-4490-3668-3 (hc)

Printed in the United States of America
Bloomington, Indiana

This book is printed on acid-free paper.

Contents

Preface

Life is filled with unanswered questions, and unfortunately as humans, we are limited in our understanding. We will never know the precise moment when the universe began. Likewise, it will most likely never be determined with absolute certainty that Lee Harvey Oswald acted alone. There are some questions, however, that can be answered through logic, reason, and deduction. These are the questions that deserve our attention while avoiding our newly developed apathy. When the subject is Theology, many people have never obtained a cognitive answer, and sadly, many never do. If the questions have a definitive answer, then a person has the inclination to believe that it may imply an ultimatum, and as we all know, nobody likes ultimatums.

In the theological world, the bigger questions generally contain several ultimatums that automatically shift a person's mindset into reverse for a safe retreat. I have spent many years studying the world's religions and have made several conclusions. My conclusions are based in what I know to be true, and even though many of my beliefs are not based in empirical knowledge, I still know them to be true. Much of what I believe is arrogated from the authority of others in whom I trust, and while this limits my understanding in lieu of firsthand knowledge, opposition based solely on disposition of secondhand knowledge will remain a moot argument for a skeptic, because we all make assumptions based on the authority of others. Through many humbling experiences, I have come to realize that I am, without a doubt, light years closer to knowing nothing than I am to knowing everything. I can, however, submit that I do know with complete certainty, particular truths and for that reason I wish to share my thoughts.

In this book, we will look at how I came to my conclusions based in reason. I will discuss my thoughts on American society and the culture as it pertains to God—from the attacks on truth in the pop culture to the attacks on history in the classrooms. I will show the inconsistencies of other popular works of theology and so-called holy books that are dependent on the postmodern thought process. I will show the stark contrast between the Christian mindset and the secular mindset that is currently at work to remove any thoughts of a deity from our society.

Placing eternity out of reach and focusing on the here and now has become the great American pastime. Since the dawn of man, questions have been asked about the very essence of life. The Egyptians, the Greeks, and the Romans all contemplated our existence and what it all meant. There is wisdom to be found in many of these ancient writings, but the inquiry didn't stop with them. Throughout the time of the prophets and the coming of the Messiah to the middle ages and right on to our grandfather's back porch, man has consistently pondered our existence. Why should we be the generation that stops asking the tougher and more prudent questions? Maybe we have a fear that our questions will be answered in a logical and reasonable manner that may require an unpleasant action. Maybe we feel we already have the answers, and to be burdened with a more logical conclusion would require a new starting point. I'm here to tell you that I don't have all the answers and that much of life will always remain a mystery. What I do have is logic, reason, and the ability to use them, along with an enormous amount of information right at my fingertips.

Bob Dylan, the great poetic icon that he is, once wrote a song entitled "Gotta Serve Somebody" following his conversion to Christianity. This idea is as true today as it always has been; by virtue of the fact that everybody serves somebody, and in many cases it is a failed attempt at serving yourself. I saw a teenager recently, wearing a T-shirt with the letters SMP embroidered on the front. It conveyed a simple message: sex, money, power. It is possible to serve any one of those vices in an attempt to serve yourself and your desires. Eventually, with time, they can consume you and become your primary purpose in life. Amazingly, most people never realize exactly what it is they are serving, and lose track of the concept that any form of worship that is not directed at the real one and only true God is a form of idolatry. Idolatry, in every case, will lead you astray, and though it may appear to be providing you self-service, it is actually leading you to destruction. No mere human or worldly possessions are worthy of our worship, but they remain the tightly gripped handlebars in too many lives. If you search your heart, you will see that you truly do serve something, even if it is just yourself or the love of a broken world.

In the end, it is up to the individual to decide what he or she believes to be true. Truth, however, is not up to the individual; it will remain a constant until the end of time. Truth is a treasure waiting to be found, and we will never find it while solely looking inward. In the same light, contrasting truths cannot be simultaneously in the same place at the same time, Therefore, when searching for the truth, always remember that to find the Ultimate Truth, many other points of view must be left to the scrap heap.

Finally, I must admit my agenda. I have but one, and that is to shed some much-needed light on the lethargic and apathetic attitudes toward searching for God and to hopefully change that attitude for as many as possible.

Introduction

Writing for me is very therapeutic. It allows me time to dwell on what matters most to me and what I consider valuable. In recent years; while mostly doing physical work; I have been at the other end of my wandering thoughts with nowhere to really place them. It might seem curious to some, but after a ten hour day of toiling in the sun my brain was often more tired than my body. Contrary to what many might think, not all contractors listen to Rock and Roll all day and dream about partying all night. I, like many others in the fields of labor, would spend much of my day thinking about true meaning, pondering my existence and debating others on similar matters. It was only when the opportunity presented itself that I finally found the time and the forum to elaborate on my ideas.

First and foremost, I will submit to you that I hold no higher degrees and that theology is my hobby, not my profession. I was never the scholarly type; in fact, I hated school. I liked playing sports and socializing, but in my formative years, the whole learning thing was pretty much lost on me. During my brief college years I had my first bitter taste of postmodern thought when I had a philosophy professor tell me that I couldn't be sure that the car I would leave in that night was the same car that I had arrived in earlier that evening. The smell of Burger King remnants that contained an eerie similarity to my breath was all the evidence I felt was needed, but he was the intellectual and I probably had a hangover. That professor—who was misguided at best but more likely bordering on insanity—had me completely fooled. I had figured at the time that he was simply trying to help his students think outside the box, and that there was no way he could actually believe in this radical skepticism. Looking back, twenty-five years later, maybe he did. Hopefully he did a 180 and came to grips with the fact that some knowledge is obtainable, including the non-empirical variety. Otherwise, he shouldn't have been administering tests with correct answers, because that would be counterintuitive to his worldview.

Based upon our modern educational system, it would then seem fitting that the skeptical people who control the academic arena are trying to remove testing altogether. Right and wrong are being debated with an emphasis on not hurting anyone's feelings, while truth is left to wander aimlessly. Today it seems that we are at liberty to believe in whatever comes down the pipe, as long as we avoid telling others that they might be wrong. Doing so would be oppressive and considered impolite, but the fact remains that we are all wrong much of the time.

It was during the late eighties that I began to develop a yearning to know a little bit more about this shared existence called life. I have since learned where that yearning stemmed from, but I don't want to get ahead of myself. Luckily, I had been born with a built-in bull detector, and most of the illogical ideology, while remotely intriguing, never really mesmerized me. I wanted to know why people believed in illusory ideology, but mostly because it appeared completely foreign to me and beyond my rationale. I would be a liar if I said that for even one minute I contemplated a conversion toward mysticism, but if I were to present an intelligent argument to the followers of Eastern thought, I needed to investigate this phenomenon that seemed to be blanketing the West.

I looked into Buddhism and Hinduism and found nothing more than an unexpected amount of absurdities. I then looked into the modern spin-offs in Eastern ideology and found their numbers to be extremely vast, but offering nothing new to the original other than clever word play. I then looked into several faith systems that borrow their foundation from Christianity. These religions were a gutted and rewired form of the original scripture, and for the life of me I can't figure out how people believe in them.

Eventually, I had come to realize that it is up to each individual to do some homework for themselves. Keep in mind; it requires reading many books to come to a logical conclusion based in reality on any particular subject. You must read around the topic and weigh it against all that you already know to be true, to allow for honest deduction. If you have trouble discerning what reality is and you're not sure if you have a foundation, then I would suggest that you see a psychiatrist. If you are a skeptic and believe that you can't know anything with any level of certainty, then you are cannibalizing yourself simply because when you submit that we can't obtain any absolutes, you are admitting that we can in the same sentence. We all have a foundation; find yours and go from there.

This book is in no way intended to stir the pot. It is not a book of us versus them, and it certainly is not a book of counting the wrongful deeds of one group and weighing them against the good deeds of another. It is, however, a book that examines human nature, the crazy-making American culture, and one person's journey to discover ultimate truth.

I have come to imagine the world as the *Titanic,* but not everyone on board realizes that the ship is sinking. The ironic part is that in reality, there are plenty of lifeboats, but people—for whatever reason—choose not to use them. In other words, it has become crystal clear to me that many people love the *Titanic* so much that they have chosen to invest their heart and soul into its grandeur, and in the end they simply choose to go down with the ship.

Most social writers are bean counters, in that they will tell you of dastardly events and the people responsible. Others will point out the outrageous words spoken by interesting personalities, while still others will use their established identity to inform you of their personal thoughts on the subject of the day. I will try my best to avoid these forums. Besides, it has been said over and over again that Jane Fonda is a traitor and that Richard Nixon was a crook. I can't speak for everyone, but I really don't care. Nixon is dead, and Jane Fonda isn't planning to visit me for tea anytime soon. If you are into counting beans and you feel as if your side has fewer rotten ones, then I suppose it might be worth your while to expose those dastardly villains.

I will plead humility and refrain from getting too nasty, because I have learned the hard way that my own indiscretions are equally on display. I will, however, do my best to explain why people say and do crazy things. I will try making sense of our apparent fear of truth and its consequences. I will appraise, hopefully with humor, our uniquely human ability to believe in obvious falsehoods. I will reveal my biased opinion of people in power who tend to pull the wool over our unsuspecting eyes, and why we allow it. Finally, I will closely examine my personal faith and how I came to have knowledge of the truth.

Chapter 1

Searching for Clues

Part 1: The Journey Begins

Like the majority of Americans, I was raised as a Christian, and like most kids during the seventies I held a deep loathing for church. Not only did I develop an aversion for church, I rebelled against my mom on Sundays because she would drag me to church. My dad was always playing golf on Sundays, and other than Christmas and his own baptism, he steered clear. My mom was raised Lutheran, as was the tradition among us Swedes, and as fate would have it, so too were my siblings and I. If you are a Catholic and church is enjoyable, then this won't make any sense, but to those who find themselves contemplating pulling the fire alarm during Mass, keep in mind that most Lutheran churches that I have attended are just as long, methodical, and boring as a Catholic Mass, only with less guilt and an absence of the emphasis on the Virgin Mary. I was the youngest of four, and by the time I turned sixteen, my mom and grandmother attended church alone. Amazingly, I learned enough to have built a foundation for my later studies, and for that I am grateful.

Love you Mom.

Part 2: Early Confusion

Growing up in the seventies in Ojai, California, was a magical time for me. We wore bell-bottom jeans, hopelessly denied that we listened to David Cassidy forty-fives, we traded baseball cards, and some of us actually caught the disco craze. Thankfully, I had two older brothers who would have pummeled me if I tried to place a Bee Gees record on the table where Led Zeppelin made its rounds. All in all, these times will always be cherished in my nostalgic mind. I had a lot of friends; I played sports and really didn't have a care in the world. Nobody close to me died, nothing tragic ever seemed to happen, and I was raised by two caring parents of opposite sexes, who provided for my every need.

In those early years, I never thought about anything beyond my own existence and when the next game was going to start. There were times in my teens when a friend or two who were more advanced in the academic arena would discuss and debate philosophical ideas, and it would always leave me bored to tears. Looking back, I realize how clueless they were and how sad it was that I was even more clueless not to notice. By the time I had graduated from high school in 1982, I had no idea what life was about and I really didn't care. I did care about my personal future and well-being, but my thought process never expanded much past money, possessions, and eventual retirement.

When my college days had come to an abrupt halt I couldn't have been any happier to be outside and free from the chalkboards and lecture halls that were enslaving me. I would love to tell you that my college days were insightful, but I have learned ten times more on my own than I did in any classroom. In the summer of 1985, I went to work for a painting contractor in Ventura, California, and I truly enjoyed the work. By 1988 I had received a contractor's license, and with a few worn-out tools and an oil-seeping Ford mini pickup truck, I started my own business. During the early years of running my company, I made plenty of money, had plenty of fun, but remained defiant to inquiring about the bigger questions in life. During these years, the political arena was heating up. It was the rise of Rush Limbaugh and the end of Ronald Reagan and Bush forty-one. It was the Clintons and their brass taking over the White House, and it seemed to divide the country in two, the liberals and the conservatives. This fight seemed to be all that people were clinging to as their fulfillment of what truly mattered. Sadly, I fell into that trap, as did most of my friends, many of whom still find their ultimate meaning in that bloodbath.

It was during my political awakening that I realized that there had to be something with more substance. Sure, there are good guys and sleazy guys; I'll leave that to you to decide. But I wanted and longed for a deeper meaning and bashing opposing ideologies for their position on the budget or some social issue just never satisfied me. Although I had desire for truth, there was a huge obstacle to overcome: I was hopelessly lazy when it came to reading and investigating. I needed a spark, and although it would take years to ignite, I got what I needed.

Part 3: Prelude to a Thought

I had a childhood friend who worked really hard in his teens and early twenties, and then decided for whatever reason to take a decade off. He worked here and there, but mostly he was just around. When I lived at the beach, he hung out at the beach. When I moved into a condo with a pool, he hung out at the pool. He had one constant habit in that he was always reading. When I came home from work, he would reveal his day's findings with his youthful enthusiasm. The conversations that ensued were one-sided and could never be considered idle chat; he was more like Dennis Miller on speed. He had stumbled onto something with substance and simply wanted to share what he had learned, and I was an easy, paint-covered target.

John Major, who by the way was never the prime minister of England, made a lot of enemies during these years. At first it appeared to be the way he presented himself in discussion that turned people away, or so it would seem, but in actuality, it was something far more convicting then his demeanor. I suppose if he had been a little gentler in his approach, it might have helped, but the real culprit wasn't how he relayed his message, it was what he was saying that made people clam up and eventually run away. John was talking about truth, and truth sheds light on every living soul and illuminates their shortcomings.

Luckily, somewhere along the way, I started to listen, and in time I came to realize that much of what John was saying made sense. At times I would defend John and his new found revelations, but mostly I wanted to deny I even knew him, in the style of the Apostle Peter. It was hard being his friend, but I loved him like a brother and for better or worse, he helped plant a seed in me that has led to my own personal journey of discovery.

Everybody has a day or two that they can remember better than others. These memories are complete with the sights and sounds and even the smells of the moment. One such occasion happened to me in 1989. I had just finished painting a large custom home in Camarillo, California. I had done my final walk-through, received my final payment, and was looking forward to some much-needed time off. It was a hot afternoon as I headed towards the pool where I knew I would find John. He would have been soaking in the hot tub if it were raining so on a 90 degree day I didn't need to channel Sherlock Holmes to know where to find him. He was alone, lying on his back, drenched in Hawaiian coconut suntan oil, reading another book. As always, he was happy to see me, because my presence meant an end to his day's solitude and the beginning of the discussion. He said that he had been praying for this one book his entire life, and in his hands he held a small, worn-out paperback edition of Dr. Hugh Ross's *The Creator and the Cosmos*. (John might be the only human being on the planet who could make a three-day-old book look like he found it in one of the great pyramids) He went on and on, explaining the contents of the book, and although I never let on that I was intrigued, I was. It intrigued me immediately.

I loved the idea of someone who could shed light on our origins and our ultimate meaning and destiny. Something inside me felt as if I was meant to know. I remember feeling a sense of anxiety flush over me as he read from that book, as it seemed to be convicting me to care. Sadly, at the time, I felt that I would never be smart enough to understand physics at that level, so I would leave it to John to help me understand. I must admit that I had a bad habit of not doing my homework on whatever new ideas were presented to me. I never learned to work on cars, because John's brother Jeff was always there to fix whatever went wrong and would soon have me back on the road. I wanted to know more about the identity of the Creator, but I just didn't want to work for it. This wasn't the first time that John had tried to push his findings my way. The documentary, *The God Makers,* which explores Mormonism in great detail, had been his first awakening as he went on and on about that for years, to mostly uninterested ears. Then there was C. S. Lewis's *Mere Christianity,* which I actually tried to read, but unfortunately, it was above my head and after one confusing chapter, I laid it down. Throughout John's discoveries, I was trailing behind, curious and longing to know more, and although I was busy I was mostly too lazy to learn

Taking information from others and running with it is as dangerous as running with scissors. I know this from experience, because I had just enough information to be dangerous. I thought that because I had learned a thing or two that made sense that I had all the answers. Well, obviously I didn't, I still don't, and I never will. But like most youngsters, I liked to pretend, and this false intellect made me feel important and useful. More than anything, it inflated my pride. There are countless people whom I encountered during these years who were forced to endure my philosophical conclusions, when in actuality I didn't have any. I was throwing half-eaten apple cores at people and expecting them to make applesauce out of it. Eventually, I started to forget the few points that I had learned, and I could no longer put them into any real context. It was then that trouble started brewing, because I would be challenged by people who knew far more than I did about what I was claiming to be an area of personal expertise. I quickly realized that the awkwardness of being exposed was far worse than any false sense of pride that I was receiving. It was time to do some homework, and I hated homework. I hated the idea of reading and investigating so much that for a period, I simply chose to remain silent and pretend to know nothing. This is an easy path to chart because people like the humility, and soon the challenging questions stopped. My personal desire to know more, however, never went away. I tried to suppress it, but it was merely dormant, and eventually the search would begin again.

Part 4: Reading ... "What a Concept"

Some years later—though not a day wiser—I still had a relentless desire for knowledge, but I hadn't really grown in my search. I did, however, have a growing business, softball games to play, golf on Sundays, and countless women to juggle. Everything I learned from Sunday school to those philosophical discussions with John remained deeply lodged in my mind (scrambled as these things were) but I wasn't ready to re-open that page. That all changed when I read the first book in the *Left Behind* series. The series was amazingly popular, and I had been given a copy by a friend who seemed to be inspired by it and thought that it might interest me. It took me a couple of months to start it, but I found it extremely entertaining, an easy read, and I couldn't wait to read the next book. I had heard of the rapture and the end times, but I never really gave it much thought, mostly to suppress the fear of the impending possible doom. I was, however, intrigued by the story and its descriptive portrayal of prophecy, and I read it to the end. Twelve books later, I had finished the series, and a new interest had developed in the whole "God thing."

I also found a new love for reading that I had never before had. I began reading anything and everything that I could find on the world views of Earth's inhabitants. In time, books that had once intimidated me were becoming my passion, and it has only grown from there. I read multiple books about the world's religions and philosophies and began weighing them against what I already knew to be true. Having a foundation to build on was instrumental to me, as I soon realized that when opening any area of study, it can be helpful to have certain presuppositions that are not up for discussion and therefore never enter into the mix. I instinctively believe that there is a God; therefore, atheism is off the table. I believe in physical reality, and nothing can permit me to believe that life is illusory. Before you label me as narrow-minded, keep in mind that we all have certain areas that remain off limits to a change of mind.

Though it will be argued by some, I believe that as humans, we are predisposed to certain ideas that are cemented into our existence. This can be easily stated in the fact that nothing that has ever been written could convince me that there is no God, and yet I haven't the time or will to read every page of literature that has ever been written. The sheer evidence of the Creation itself is all I need to disregard contrary ideas, and the works of the world's greatest skeptics have done little to dissuade me.

It has been twenty-plus years since I started my inquiries, and I have read hundreds of books on theology, including the ones that once challenged me. Although I am merely a layman, I have added to my earlier conclusions of there being a God and that the physical realm is real. In later chapters, I will discuss these findings in greater detail, but for now I'm more focused on shedding light on the society as a whole, what we generally believe, and why we believe it.

Chapter 2

Church Is Flat-out Boring

Part 1: The Traditional American Church

There are so many denominations of the Christian faith that it is hard to keep track of their names, and the subtle differences in the traditions of each. The main tenets of the Christian belief system are for the most part cherished and protected in their teaching, but until the recent rise of non-denominational contemporary churches, most American churches held one common denominator: they were boring. People are hard to reach when they are bored to tears and their only inclination to attend is to be dutiful and eat cookies. I mentioned before that I was raised in a traditional Lutheran church, and that sheer boredom drove me away. My childhood church had one organ player who played at a laggard pace, and the time set aside for worship through song was limited to uplifting words set to the tone of a dirge.

We had two readings from the gospel by church members who would quietly walk to the pulpit, read the words, and just as quietly return to their seats. There was zero discussion of these readings and no instruction or teaching as to what they meant. It was as if they were reading a death sentence rather than the intended message of life and joy. Meanwhile, the congregation would have phantom itches on their left arms as they checked their watches and cleverly hid their yawns. The sermon was always a moral that came from somewhere in the Bible, but none of us knew where and nobody seemed to care other than the fact that it was usually twenty minutes long and the countdown to the exiting had begun.

I can't speak for everyone, and I realize that the traditions are varied throughout the different denominational churches in twentieth-century America, but generally I think it is safe to say that many churches and their pastors, elders, and teachers have done a poor job of keeping our attention. People of faith in every congregation should be equating their attendance with a good time. People should want to go to church for reasons completely separate from duty and a release of conscience. Church on Sunday should be uplifting, thought-provoking, and basically a sanctuary from the outside world. What should be more pleasing than spending time with God and learning of his purpose and our place in his plan? Sadly, many traditional denominations of the Christian faith have lost the idea of conveying the message of the Good News in an elevated manner and have instead instituted a man-made structure of worship that is repetitive, boring, and currently increasing the National Football League's television ratings tenfold.

My cousin Mike attended a traditional church as a child that had a large, open-beam wooden ceiling, and when the temperature would reach ninety degrees or above, the agitation from boredom was enhanced with perspiration and odor. Luckily for twelve-year-old little Mikey, his dad was a contractor and volunteered to install roof ventilations that could open the ceiling to the skies above and allow the heat to escape with the help of the exterior wind-driven fans. Mike's dad had spent a few Saturdays working on the roof and finally the church members had some relief from the stale, hot air that added to their annoyance. On the first Sunday with open skies visible from the pews, the children were asked to leave for Sunday school when the sermon was about to begin. It was then that Mikey decided to take a detour. His dad had mentioned that he would need his help loading the twenty-four-foot extension ladder that remained leaning on the side of the church when the service was over and Mikey, while on his detour, thought it would be cool to climb the ladder and look down at the people inside as they were hearing their day's moral. Mikey had spent the previous forty minutes looking up at the blue skies through the opening, praying to God. He wasn't praying for salvation or the well-being of others; he was most likely praying for a bird or a swarm of bees to enter the church and interrupt the service to relieve his boredom.

When Mikey covertly made his way to the opening and peered down, he could see his parents listening to the remotely biblical message, and others who were fighting to keep their eyes open. After a moment or two, a diabolical thought crossed his mind and he couldn't keep himself from implementing his plan. Mikey put his hands on both sides of his mouth and in the loudest, deepest voice that his twelve-year-old frame could muster, he shouted, "This is God!" and quickly ducked out of view. As he sat there and listened, he could hear people shuffling about and the panic of a few. A moment later, before anyone had realized what was happening, he again shouted through the opening, "I said, this is God!" Several of the elderly people in the congregation nearly passed out in confusion, and the service had come to a screeching halt. The gig was up, however, as Mikey's dad was rounding the church building faster than Jesse Owens, and Mikey was headed for deep trouble.

This is the sole memorable day in Mike's early church years, and he doesn't attend church regularly anymore, at least to my knowledge. Years later, that incident that freed the congregation from their shackles, if only for a moment, is probably remembered with glee and gratitude. If learning about God is not allowed in the public square and if our parents have lost interest due to tiresome services, then generations will follow who have zero inclination to understand God's purpose. Luckily for all of us, the rise of the contemporary church is in full force and is beginning to bring people back from the abyss.

Part 2: The Contemporary Church

Most contemporary churches are non-denominational, but many traditional denominational churches have followed suit in the new format. In these newfound places of worship, organ-playing and choirs have been replaced with electric guitars, acoustic guitars, pianos, and drums. The music is led by worship teams who rehearse on a regular basis and present uplifting worship in the form of songs with a beat. People are found to be dressed casually, smiling, and generally enjoying the atmosphere. The message is read from the Bible with a teaching that helps the congregation understand the meaning of the Word, while never avoiding the woes contained therein. Many modern churches have extravagant luncheons that follow each service, where people can relax in comfortable settings and have fellowship with other believers. This is a far cry from the cookies and fruit punch that eight or nine people enjoyed following my early church days, when the discussion would ensue about which church member wasn't attending regularly.

This format is now commonplace among the more modern church model, and it is leading to a renewal of the Christian Church as a whole. What was once a dreaded appearance is now looked forward to by many and at least more tolerated by others. If going to heaven and meeting God is enlightening and fills you with joy, then going to a place of worship should be a happy place where you are fed spiritually. The sad realization is that many baby boomers that have left the church have never experienced a contemporary church and are left with images of being bored to tears and filled with morals that they might just as well have learned from a nursery rhyme.

Church elders who once ruled the grounds with an iron fist have been replaced by caring elders and youth pastors who are often heard saying much more than "Stop messing around" or "Shushhhh!" Basically, the pride that once infiltrated the most astute of attendees has been reversed in the knowledge that we are but one body of believers, and that their finely pressed suit and solemn look are not helping anybody's cause. Pastors in the contemporary churches are at liberty to usher in humor and anecdotes to their message, but in most cases teach straight from the Bible. Sunday school has evolved into a place that isn't quite as dreadful either. While there is still a much-needed message relayed, it is surrounded with songs, crafts, and humor as well. For the older kids, church is led by youth pastors who gear their music toward the younger attendees, and the message, while taken from a biblical stance, is relevant to their age and understanding. It is amazing to see the younger crowd actually seem happy to be at church, especially when I think back to my early days, when the very mention of church had me faking whatever illness was currently going around.

The traditional American church needed a makeover, and thankfully it got one. If you haven't been to church in a while, find a contemporary one and you might actually enjoy it. These are not hard to find; they are usually filled with large crowds of happy people who attend because they actually want to be there, and who have long lost the idea of it being their duty and sole responsibility to do so.

Part 3: The Next Step

Christian retreats are a great way to make new friends and enjoy whatever setting in which you find yourself. Most retreats are held in rural areas where there are many outdoor activities to keep the people busy between periods of worship and messages. While retreats are a great way to get away from life's worries and to refocus our attention on God, I've often wondered why modern churches don't follow this recipe every Sunday. Is it really necessary to drive four hours into the mountains to keep the attention of followers by involving them in adventurous activities? I realize that resources are limited in every church across the land, but more can be done to make Sunday a day of worship, learning, fellowship, and several forms of activities. Church has come a long way, but the final ingredient that might bring more people to the table is after-church activities.

Whether it is a softball game, a picnic at the park, a field trip to fish a local river, or all three, make Sunday a day of fun that is spent together with other believers. Most people go home, mow their lawn, and fall asleep on Sunday afternoon. Why not make every Sunday a retreat from our daily worries and increase the fellowship that so many are lacking, especially among some of the larger, more intimidating churches. If you love the time of worship with the energized music and you look forward to a weekly message that is read from the Bible, then what could be better than participating with like-minded people every Sunday in an activity that you love to do?

A quick announcement at the beginning of a Sunday morning service will direct attendees toward the day's activities. If only a few people make an appearance to fish a local river, then they will have made a few new friends while being in a relaxed setting in which to share their testimonies and concerns. Small groups meet for study, fellowship, and food in every corner of the country, but adding an activity that alleviates the anxious feelings of a formal gathering is the missing link. Christians need to get involved, and when a reclusive person is comfortably brought to the forefront while having newfound allies in their venture from the couch, a transition will often occur.

Just a Thought #1

Everybody fantasizes about being able to go back in time, maybe to avoid an unpleasant moment or have a second chance to make the game-winning shot. Sometimes I fantasize about being little Bobby Segotta again, sitting in the pews of my childhood church. Yes, it's true; I was once a skinny little tow-head with bright blue eyes. I also had a problem with reoccurring snot, but that's another story altogether. Anyway, I would love to have the chance to stand up after the reading of the first or second gospel and say, "What exactly did Jesus mean when he said that?" This, of course, would upset the routine and probably force one of the stern elders to stare me down and proclaim, "This is not the time or place for open discussion, young man" To which I would reply with the mind of a forty-five-year-old, "Look, just because God obviously forgot to give you an inquiring mind doesn't mean he didn't give me one."

Chapter 3

What Were You Thinking?

Part 1: Crazy-making

Noam Chomsky, the left leaning political activist believes that it is astonishing that there are large segments of the American population that believe in miracles performed by God and in the physical resurrection of Christ. He is also amazed that the numbers of believers are not duplicated anywhere else in the world.

He's right. It is astonishing. It is also astonishing that we are the most generous population and the most advanced and the most prosperous. Americans have many shortcomings, but Noam should see the correlation between what we believe and what we produce. Sheer hatred of divinity will blind even the brightest among us.

I've always marveled at some of the crazy ideas that people come up with and their ability to truly believe in obvious falsehoods. I met a girl some years ago who had paid a thousand dollars to attend a series of seminars in the L.A. area about the true meaning of things. I liked the sound of that, so I asked her what she was learning. She said, and I quote, "This guy, he comes out and says that everything I'm about to tell you is true, but then again, it might also be false; it all depends on you." The astonishing part was the excitement in her voice while she practically glowed while offering her description. Well, obviously I could have been six years old and still have known *that* was ridiculous. I simply told her that she was being scammed and that she should save her money for the shrink sessions that she would surely need if she continued thinking crazy. It did, however, make me think. Do people actually believe that truth is relative? Yes they do, and their numbers are growing.

All across the academic world, any topic that can't be explained through physics is now "personal perspective." In fact, some believe that you can't know anything at all. If I wanted to explain this thought process from the beginning, we would need to examine pre-modern thought, modern thought, to the now predominant postmodern thought. It's a long, drawn-out process and although crucial to a full understanding of relative truth, it is not my desire to delve to deep here. I would suggest that you pick up some books at your local library and see for yourself if the curiosity propels you. There is a reason you believe what you believe, and I can guarantee you that your thought process has been greatly affected by this lineage of thinking. It is sad but true that we are drifting away from truth in our textbooks right into our Sunday papers. I never really got to know that girl, as she was only a friend of a friend, and I might have only seen her one more time in passing, but I've often wondered what happened to her. Did she continue floundering through absurdities? Did she give up on finding solidified ground and make her own hand-picked world view? Or did she find her way to the truth?

I'll admit that the seminar girl was an anomaly at the time, but in the late nineties I met another girl, whom I dated for more than a year. The relationship became more of a science project after the first month or so, because I couldn't believe how far removed from reality she was. We came from completely different backgrounds. I had the typical upbringing from what most would consider normal parents, where as she had been raised by a hippie father and an apathetic mother, while her grandfather—who happened to be gay—was the "great patriarch" of the family. Her uncle was a prep school teacher whom she thought was brilliant and enlightened because he didn't own a TV and refrained from eating red meat. She was a smart, sweet, educated person who was more confused than Daffy Duck on Quaaludes. To say that she was left of center was the equivalence of placing Omaha, Nebraska in the same general vicinity as the Hawaiian Islands. She had been born with a huge heart, but unfortunately, I wasn't one to say that her heart was in the right place, because it wasn't. It was lost in space with Buck Rogers and she had no intention of retrieving it. She wasn't just another seeker on the wrong tracks, she was a true believer, and her belief was entrenched in skepticism. She hated religion because it didn't shine a very bright light on her relatives, and in time she grew to hate me for pointing that out to her.

Our relationship came to an end when she and her comrades started telling me that my perception of what was true didn't necessarily make it true. Okay, I can dance with that, but only to a point. When it comes to reality that is not beyond physics, we're going to have a problem. We had a huge fight via e-mail, and amazingly, she still found herself heading to my house for a night out. I remember thinking about the crazy-making statements that she was trying to imply while I was awaiting her arrival. I remember thinking about the silly idea of relative truth, when suddenly I realized that my old buddy John had said many times before that if a person doesn't believe in right and wrong, just take their wallet and they'll quickly change their tune. Such a devilish scheme couldn't go unimplemented. So when she arrived, we made our peace over a glass of beer and we were ready to hit the town. As we were headed toward the door, I asked to see her purse, and after a couple of "whys," she relented. I simply took her purse, threw it on my bed, locked the bedroom door, and said, "Are you ready to go?" Confusion set in and she went from inquiring to demanding her purse back in a matter of minutes, of course I simply denied knowing anything about the whereabouts of her purse. In anger, she finally shouted, "I saw you throw it on your bed and lock the door," to which I replied, "That is your version of what happened, not mine."

Needless to say, I had popped her preposterous balloon, and she never trusted me again. The relationship ended shortly thereafter, and she finally admitted that I constantly made her feel stupid, which of course, was my intention. I never saw much good that could come from being sympathetic to irrational thought.

I learned a lot from that relationship. I had infiltrated the camp of a true believer in radical thought, and I have to say it was an amazing time, Frustrating, but insightful. I later apologized for my behavior, because I was a jerk and had said many hurtful things, and although I could have shown more compassion, I stand by what I said. I've always known that there were many people out there with crazy thoughts, but I had never before been in the front row with a clear, unobstructed view. Most people don't lean toward radical thought on either side of the aisle, but we are certainly influenced by it, and it wears down our thinking until we begin to make concessions away from what we do believe. Abortion, homosexual adoption, and explicit sexual content on TV are commonplace today, but these perversions would have caused our grandparents to riot in the streets fifty years ago. Today, personal choice is more cherished and protected than what we choose. It is a sad time to see our society move in the obviously wrong direction, and though it is not a mystery why it is happening, turning a blind eye is what will remain the ultimate mystery. Sometimes I want to bang my head against the wall when I see a large portion of the population with zero desire to understand anything beyond their own personal existence. One of the major tenets of postmodern thought is that ultimate truth is unobtainable and more importantly, undesired. So how did we get here and where is it leading us?

Just a Thought #1

Atheism is on the rise in America, and these secular skeptics are forming well-organized publicity machines. They scorn the very idea of believing in any form of a deity and will be quick to replace the desire for God with a state-run religious ideology. Amazingly, these so-called proponents of science forgot to do their math. A quick look into physics will show the actual numbers, but to put it into simple terms, the odds of there not being a creator is an equation that would scare even the most hardened gambler and should be a wakeup call to the so-called enlightened skeptic.

Part 2: Skeptical Leaps of Faith

Either God wants to abolish evil, and cannot; or he can, but does not want to; or he can cannot and does not want to. If he wants to, but cannot, he's impotent. If he can and does not want to, he's wicked. But, if God both can and wants to abolish evil, then how come there is evil in the world?

Epicurus, philosopher

God both can and will abolish evil, but not until he gives the perpetrators of said evil time to repent. Remember, God didn't create evil; he allowed us to partake in evil. Without God, we would have pure evil at every turn. With God, we have a way out from evil.

The skeptical thought process is nothing new. Read the works of Kant and Nietzsche to begin your search. We are all influenced by the thinking of certain secular forefathers who, more than anything, were looking for a way out, as they wanted to be hidden from truth to avoid accountability. There are so many works on the subject that it could take a lifetime to examine just a taste of the anti-theistic movement. I'm here to tell you that there is nothing new under the sun (I borrowed that line from God) and that you will find one underlying similarity in all these skeptics: they all seek to find a way out. Most people who deny a deity rely on Darwin to explain our origins and everything that follows. It takes a giant leap of faith to believe in the naturalistic explanation for our origin, and it gets more improbable the further it goes. I realize that Darwin is considered a god in the academic arena, but the denial of God himself is a revered concept as well. Go figure. Hitler and Stalin held true to their belief in evolution and slaughtered millions while simply weeding out the less fit. J.R.R. Tolkien and C. S. Lewis snapped out of their belief in evolution and became two of the more creative and insightful writers of their time. Go figure again.

If life began with a lightning bolt striking a primordial soup to form amino acids, the building blocks of life, then where did the lightning bolt originate? Who made the soup, for that matter? Was there a can of Campbell's cream of mushroom handy at the dawn of time? The explanations and added theories to evolution only get more absurd from there; look it up. So why do so many people of our generation avoid the bigger questions, and put all their stock in whatever can make them feel happy and content? We do this, to put it in the simplest of terms, because it is in our nature to seek a way out as well. A fifteen-year-old child could never be happier than the first time he is left home alone for a weekend. Generally, they will do the things that they could never do, while in the watchful eyes of their parents and most of these acts will not be in their best interest. Autonomy is a cherished idea, especially when there are no consequences. We learn at an early age that there are consequences to our actions, but we seem to have forgotten or choose to believe that there is no consequence beyond this life. It narrows down the responsibility to the here and now, and that just makes life easier, or so it would seem.

Famous skeptics are well read. In fact, they are so well read that they have anointed themselves as judge and jury to the metaphysical realm. James A. Haught is a noted atheist and author who has written many books illustrating his world view, which contains an obvious detestation for religion. In one of his later books, *2000 Years of Disbelief,* Haught documents the views of many famous non-believers and includes segments of their writings and quotations to further his case. Being famous certainly doesn't make a person more enlightened than others, but in our culture it does incur a curiosity within the reader due to our illogical love affair with people in the limelight. Haught uses these icons to form his assault, which is based on empirical knowledge but he offers little to those seeking answers with any real substance. The persons and their views depicted in this book range from Kurt Vonnegut Jr to Mark Twain, from George Bernard Shaw to Ayn Rand along with many others.

2000 Years of Disbelief contains several quotes from many famous people from various backgrounds. It also contains a short biography of each individual that we are meant to be in awe with, but the quotations and biographies are missing a key ingredient: answers! Each subject has a plethora of comments on why a believer might be wrong to have faith, but offers little, if anything, in the way of an alternative. We've all heard the term *intellectual idiot,* and this book displays a multitude of them. Something happens to people when they reach the point where the idea of learning ends and their focus shifts to lecturing others on their wisdom. Each person discussed in this book has overachieved in their particular field; they are smart and respected by all accounts, but they snicker at the idea of a true deity while foregoing true debate.

Currently, we see respected elitists making their rounds from campus to campus, getting paid handsomely for speaking engagements. They tell you *"how it is"* and then head home to bask in their own greatness while resting assured that they have moved beyond the point of being challenged. College professors worship at the feet of these speakers, because in reality that is who they aspire to be. A young boy might dream of saving the girl and finding the treasure, where as a college professor might dream of a day where he has the pulpit firmly in hand while everyone in attendance stares with adoring eyes. This explains why they are so authoritative in the classroom; they are merely practicing for their dream job, where challenge is negated altogether.

Ben Stein recently made a movie about intelligent design entitled *Expelled,* in which he traveled to several sites, including many campuses, and asked some basic questions about our origin to the *"most enlightened among us."* The movie is hysterical, as is Ben Stein, and it proves the point I'm trying to make. Stein challenges his subjects to provide an alternative to intelligent design that is both plausible and provable. Obviously, they have a huge problem in doing so, and Stein eventually makes them feel awkward and stupid as only he knows how. Basically, Stein challenged them to present a cognitive answer while defusing their authoritative nature, and the results were as expected: they imploded. There is a reason why so many avoid *The O'Reilly Factor,* and Bill is lobbing softballs the size of watermelons compared to the questions that I would like to ask some of these knuckleheads. I doubt that we will soon see Tom Cruise debating Josh McDowell on matters of theology, because his priorities will find him in a safe haven, answering questions about his cat while lounging on the couch with the *View* gals.

If Kurt Vonnegut, Jr. were to have had a discussion with C. S. Lewis about religion and our origins, it might have gone something like this:

Lewis: Where did we come from?

Vonnegut: Well, we certainly didn't come from a jealous and vengeful God that is described as such in your Bible.

Lewis: I realize that the words of the scripture have little bearing on your world view, but that wasn't the question. I asked, where did we come from?

Vonnegut: Whether it is natural order or divine intervention is not the point. Realizing the atrocities and social ills perpetrated by the Church for over two thousand years is unavoidable.

Lewis: So you're saying that you don't know.

Vonnegut: I'm saying that I know that you are wrong, and until we evolve to an understanding that these silly superstitions are the very shackles that enslave us, we will remain unable to be progressive in our growth.

Lewis: But where did we come from?

Vonnegut: (Silence with an angry frown.)

The smarter a person becomes, the less he is challenged by others. The less he is challenged by others, the smarter he thinks he is. The smarter he thinks he is, the greater the pride and ego will inflate. When the pride and ego inflate to the point where humility is lost, all perspective will be lost as well. When people lose all perspective, they become elitists in their field of expertise and can then be dubbed as *"intellectual idiots"* who are mostly unable to debate contrasting ideas to their own because their ideas are permanently engraved in their minds as being right.

Part 3: Don't be too Proud

Pride is the true culprit in our flawed personalities. C. S. Lewis said that pride is from hell itself, and a quote from *Mere Christianity* puts this idea into focus: "Nothing makes a man feel more prideful and powerful than to be able to move other men around like toy soldiers." Unfortunately, we all have this problem. It is more than just an annoying tidbit in our character to be dealt with, it is our very own wrecking ball set on destroying us. Pride loves any idea that will send us toward a false sense of freedom. Freedom from poverty is a good thing, but if we take a prideful stance on our rise from poverty and allow that pride to swell, then we would be better left in poverty. Pride will also lead us toward autonomy, and that will lead us astray from where our heart desires to go. Nobody loves the self-righteous and nobody loves the hopelessly arrogant, and yet we all want to be loved.

When you take pride to an extreme level, it becomes even more damaging. If you become self-righteous and arrogant, and you begin to play people like toy soldiers, you will be entering into enemy territory. In doing so, you may become rich and powerful, and it may even invoke great self-satisfaction, but it will come crashing down like thunder at some point. In some twisted way, you may find temporal peace during your rise to glory, but when your pride rises up to deny you a relationship with God, you will most likely replace that much needed relationship with either yourself or somebody else who is non deserving. Most manmade ideology has a constant and recurring theme: you're in charge, you know best, and you are self-contained. Look at today's advertisements and tell me that they are not catering to your ego with every click of the remote. Most assuredly, this is what the skeptical thinkers have been lobbying for all along. As long as they continue to cater to a man's pride and ego, they will eventually possess the man.

The story is as old as the Garden of Eden and has been played out in the form of reruns throughout history. If a large group of academic elitists wish to increase their numbers, all that is needed is to make a person believe that the party wouldn't be the hot spot that it currently is without their amazing presence. In other words, cater to their pride and ego, throw in an extremely suspect explanation for their existence that negates responsibility, and bingo, they will have recruited true believers.

There is a reason that many politicians will lie, cheat, or steal to keep their seat at the table of power: they have been self-anointed to a prestigious position through pride and they have become addicted to the attributes contained therein. Power through humility equals production and compassion, whereas power through pride equals obstruction and oppression. Read the words and study the actions of today's leaders and you will quickly see who is being led astray by their destructive pride and who is remaining humble.

The best way to illustrate this point is in a quick painting lesson that may be useful to you at some point while sprucing up your home. I have several friends who are painting contractors, as am I. Throughout the years, we have shared employees, tools, and even our personal skills when one or another has time limits on a particular project. It is obvious that when you have two or more people working on a project who have become accustomed to being in charge, a battle of wills might ensue. One such incident occurred a few years back when I was helping a friend meet a time schedule on a set of interior condominium remodels. I was enameling windows in the bedrooms while I watched my friend re-assembling the closet poles and brackets. He had taken the poles off the brackets, removed the brackets, sprayed the closets, primed and painted the poles by hand, and was now putting everything back together. I noticed that the brackets were yellowed and rusted to a point, and when the assembly was complete, the freshly painted closet—complete with the poles that were painted in the exact same paint—looked sad to be in the presence of the discolored, worn-out brackets. I made a quick suggestion that in the future, it would look better and save a great deal of time to use a spray can of primer on the brackets and the poles and then spray the entire closet at once. This didn't go over very well, and he later made the comment that working with me was a complete nightmare because of my intrusion upon his way of doing things.

I would be a liar if I said that I have never been on the opposite side of that equation, but hopefully I have learned a thing or two over the years. It would be obvious to most that my suggestion made sense—easier, more efficient, and a cleaner, better-looking final project. Pride had made an appearance that day, and it led to an obstruction of production and an oppression of an idea. If pride had taken a backseat, it would have led to better production and compassion to the person with the idea. I was made to feel bad for offering a suggestion because it wasn't my place to make one. Prima donnas come in every shape and size, and I've acted the part way too many times myself, but it has been my recognition of such that is slowly freeing me from this hindrance.

Part 4: Pride's Conclusion

Not all people are skeptics, but a large portion of society live their lives with little care or knowledge about things beyond their physical understanding. Paying their bills and raising their kids are what matter most. Fun and excitement is a close second, and retirement is their later concern. Beyond those realities, life—if it has any meaning at all—is not important enough to examine. So why have we become so lethargic and apathetic? Because for many of us, it appears to be the easy, no-questions way to avoid truth. Some people prefer the answer that a dead scientist has offered in the form of a theory to the bigger questions, and the modern-day followers of the theory will lie to you at every turn to keep this deception alive and well. Some are pushing an agenda and some are true believers, but they all share in their aversion for those who oppose them and to this point, it is their own personal pride that is a blinding flash in the eyes of reason.

Part 5: Creation Lovers

Before I expand on the absurdities of holding the creation in greater esteem than the Creator himself, I need to tell you a story. Everybody has a story or two that has become legendary, and this particular story has been told and retold more times than I can count. I'm always asked to tell the story whenever I'm around someone who has heard the story and has a new and eager listener at the ready. It's a tad bit graphic, so be warned.

Several years ago, a friend of mine had a cat that had a large litter of kittens. Without asking, he brought one over to my house and simply stated that I needed one. It was a cute kitten, orange with white feet and fluffy soft fur. I was a big Broncos fan at the time, and I named him Elway in honor of old number 7. Elway took to me right away, because I think he was taken from his mother a little early and thought of me as his papa. He would literally run to me every time I came home and would follow me wherever I went throughout the house. Elway hadn't been in his new home more than a month when suddenly he disappeared. I was dating an animal lover at the time named Kristen who couldn't quite be labeled an activist, but she was leaning over the fence to become one. She had me put flyers up all over the neighborhood, in the hope that someone would find Elway and return him to his home.

Several days went by, and Elway appeared to be gone for good. Then one Sunday afternoon, as Kristen and I were watching a sappy PBS program on television, a friend stopped by to use my punching bag that was hanging in the garage. We could hear him huffing and puffing away in there for all of about five minutes, when suddenly it went silent. I remember saying, "Ahh, he probably had a heart attack, I'll check on him when the show is over." That thought had just left my mind when the back door opened and I saw my sweaty friend walking toward us. Being of the inquisitive nature, I had to wonder why his hands were behind his back. He had a horrified look on his face and he said in a withdrawn voice, "I'm not so sure you guys want to see this." In retrospect, he was right, but he showed us anyway. When he pulled his hand out from behind his back, there was Elway. He had literally been scalped. The fur and skin on top of his head had been peeled back into a tight roll, and all that was left on the top of his head was a thin layer of dried blood that enabled us to see the entire bone on top of his skull. We're not talking about a small area; it was complete from the top of the eye lids to the back of his ears. Elway was a mess, and before I could even react, Kristin started to cry.

Curiously, and most relevant to my story, there was one of those roly-poly sow bugs stuck smack dead in the middle of the thin layer of hardened blood on the top of his head. He appeared to have been making a trek across the head when the blood hardened and he got stuck like a kid playing in cement. The bug was dead, but nobody present wanted to touch it, so for the time being, the bug remained as an ornament. My friend had found Elway curled up next to the washing machine, and we have since concluded that he must have been inside the back of the machine when a particular cycle led to his dismay. Elway didn't seem to be in much pain; he just seemed dazed.

Of course with Kristen in the mix, we had to take him to Urgent Animal Care because they are the only place open on a Sunday. The whole way there, I kept thinking that they would take one look at him and recommend putting him to sleep, and the little guy looked like that would have been his recommendation as well. When we arrived, there was only one person in the waiting room and two animal nurse people behind the counter. The reaction from all three was entirely as expected: a step back, hands over the face, the whole enchilada. When the nurse finally composed herself, she said, "That is the most horrifying thing that I have ever seen," to which I replied, "I know, it is horrifying, but if we can get this darn cat away from my sow bug, I swear we can revive him." I thought it was funny. I still think it's funny. In fact, I'd say it was one of the funniest things I've ever said, as it was unrehearsed and a simple attempt to lighten the mood. It didn't go over nearly as well with the original hearers as it does with those who hear the story second hand. These women were ready to kill me, barbecue me, and have me for dinner. That one comment ended my relationship with Kristen, because she couldn't see the difference between an insensitive person and one who was trying to soften the mood. That, of course, was her problem. The veterinarian simply rinsed off Elway's head and gave us a topical solution and informed us that he might live. He too seemed afraid to remove the bug, and it wasn't until we applied the first coat of his medicine that the bug was finally removed.

Elway had lost his whiskers and therefore his balance, and for the next several weeks, he would run into walls and chair legs. This was horrible because his bony head would make that "toink" noise that made everyone in the house wince. A few weeks later, Elway was gone for good. Deep down, I know what happened to him, but the person who used his 22 caliber rifle to put Elway out of his misery has yet to fess up.

I'll never understand with complete certainty the mentality of people who put all their stock in the created world. I love trees and animals as much as the next guy, but is it a crime to love people more? Show me a radical environmentalist or a radical animal-rights activist and I'll show you somebody with a past, and human relationships are usually not their strong point. Becoming radical in anything will set you apart from the remaining logical-thinking public, and never in a good way. The mentality of a radical would change drastically if the scales tipped in the other direction and the company in their cause began to rise. If a radical animal-rights advocate had his way and everyone suddenly took his identical stance, it would not end his radical nature. He would merely move on to a new cause. Eventually, if time allowed, he would be forced to become radical against his initial cause, to remain set apart. I realize that would never happen in one lifetime, but if time permitted, he would come full circle; having pride in their unique positions is in their nature.

In the same light, broken relationships with other human beings will tend to push people away from God, because communicating with each other is how we learn to communicate with a higher power. This is why we must learn to forgive and mend these relationships in order to steer ourselves away from these radical tendencies. Not only is it a good idea, it is a command.

God created the earth and gave *man* dominion over all its inhabitants. Ever wonder why he would grant us the responsibility? Why would he make us more important than a lima bean? Why should we have any more right to live than the chicken we just ate? There is an understanding to this crazed position that can be found by simple reason. If the creation is a reflection of the Creator, which it is, then we need to rethink the creation and honor the purpose of the Creator.

Chaining yourself to a tree to protect it is ridiculous, because although you can hug a tree all day long, the tree will never hug you back, and it surely won't enlighten you to unfound mysteries. When you stare into the trunk of a tree and worship it, you are looking away from God, who is standing next to the tree and wondering why you are not worshipping him. If you want to see the greatest of his reflections, then look in the mirror, but don't look too long, because you too are just a reflection. We are to be good stewards of the planet, and although I have no problem killing and eating a chicken, I believe that eating free-range chickens is more humane. Likewise, I have no problem using timber to build homes for shelter, but to be good stewards, we must always replant, and for the most part we do. Being destructive of our own home is never a good idea, but ignoring our resources and refusing to use them is offensive to the provider.

Our unique ability to communicate with our Creator is what sets us apart from all other species, and places us in the realm of accountability. Everything else, the animals, mountains, oceans, and space, are not to be abused but to be admired as God's great glory. We are, however, to make use of all resources in a way that pleases God. The use of natural resources is a topic that can be discussed and debated, but to radically defend the creation and ignore the Creator is truly a sad state to be living in.

Just a Thought #2

Being proud has its place. You can be proud of a son or daughter serving in the military, and rightfully so. Forgoing the Creator, however, and not giving *him* the praise for your feeling of pride, puts all the glory on you. Whatever you are currently proud of will eventually consume you without balancing it with a humble attitude toward God.

Chapter 4

"The After-retirement Blues"

Part 1: When Good People Neglect

Living forty years in one place, I've come to know a lot of people. I've met some strange people, whom I touched on earlier, but even more intriguing to me are the so-called normal people. After I married my wife Chris, we abruptly moved to the Northwest to be closer to family and to purchase warm jackets. It is a long and boring story, but for better or worse, we are here. Financially, things could be better, but my wife's amazing love has been a rock in my life. Kyle, my stepson, can be the most challenging child in certain areas, but to me, he is the greatest kid that I have ever loved. He has developed his own pace in life, and though it can be frustrating at times, he has always been respectful and will always give his best for my approval. For the most part, it has been the three of us drudging through the gray skies up here, attempting to stay dry and warm. We've made some friends along the way, but I've found that making friends isn't quite as easy when you get older. I still remain close to my childhood chums and we speak frequently over the phone and on occasion we will get together when time permits.

Most of my friends do the "life thing" really well. They have successful careers and businesses; they raise their children with quality values and are respected members of their communities. Oddly, most of them never give more than an inkling of thought to what they're going to do after retirement. We all know that ten out of ten people die, and when push comes to shove, most people will say that they believe in some form of God simply to stop the troubling questions of the inquisitor. Frankly, most of my friends have no idea who God really is. I hate to say it, but it would appear as if they feel that the bigger questions are best answered by the academic scholars with their skeptical outlook. Most of the people I know never even talk to their children about a higher power. Ironically, they are conservative in their thinking and lay claims that they wouldn't trust the educational system as far as they could throw it, but on the subject of God, it is probably best left to someone else.

For the past few years I have had a young apprentice working with me. He is twenty years old and he actually followed my family and me from Southern Oregon to Seattle in search of better prospects in the painting business. He has been a quiet listener to all my ranting for some time now, and in return, I have learned a lot about him and his family. He has a close family environment, and he cherishes his time spent with them; by most standards, they seem to be honest, hard-working people. Last spring, as he was preparing to go camping with his family for an Easter celebration, I asked him, out of nowhere, if he knew the true meaning of Easter and sadly he had no idea. I was blown away by this revelation, because I knew that he had celebrated Easter for at least fifteen years that he could remember, and other than the Easter bunny and the hunting of eggs, he was clueless to the actual meaning. Sadly, nobody ever told him what Easter was all about, and it got me thinking—did his parents know? If he could reach twenty years of age and not know the true meaning of the Easter celebration, I suppose it is possible to reach forty years of age and be clueless to a commonly known fact. Are Christians that lethargic? What about Muslims, Mormons, and Hindus, are they neglecting their religion too? Something inside me says no. I stated earlier that 80 percent of Americans claim to be Christian, but how many of them know much, if anything, about the tenets of their stated belief?

Part 2: Politically Dimwitted

It has been said that you shouldn't talk politics and religion at the dinner table. Well, that might be true if the guests do not share the same faith or political view, but if you're having a dinner party for the PETA executives, then talking politics will be a given. Likewise, if you are having brunch with fellow Hindus, then other than candles and sandals, religion will probably dominate the discussion. Apparently, political correctness has partially outlawed the idea of teaching our kids anything worth knowing, in lieu of politeness and so-called tolerance. Besides, when an entire generation has been slipping by and the people of that generation mostly neglect asking the pertinent questions themselves, then how are they expected to relay a cognitive answer? We are currently raising a generation of kids who seem to have no desire to learn about a possible Creator, and therefore the question remains: where will they turn if they suddenly develop a desire to know?

I receive many phone calls from friends and family on a daily basis, and I always marvel at the simplicity of the dialect. It is great to know how everyone is—all the stories, all the achievements; it's always good and exciting to hear from other people. Faith is easily and openly discussed with people who believe as I do, but to some, the topic of faith is the ultimate buzz kill. Not so ironically, it is the people who are winning the game of life who are the hardest to reach. It is as if reaching their worldly goals is the ultimate prize and therefore, money, possessions, and achievements dominate these conversations. For many, it really is a human race and they are hell-bent on winning it. Political awareness is the depth scale of these conversations, and anything beyond that realm is mere pleasantries.

I believe that all people have a longing for substance and that somewhere deep inside of all of us, we want the more prudent questions answered. Along the way, many people conclude that truth probably can't be known with any certainty, and therefore give up the search and focus on the here and now, or they find a suitable answer based on something unreasonable that at the time made sense to them. Most people I know fall into one of these two categories of self-denial, and they seem content with allowing this aspect of their lives to remain idle.

Oddly, most claim to be Christians, which to me is the equivalent of being a vegetarian who avoids vegetables. If a person has a faith-based world view, it would make sense to explore their faith from time to time. If you are not sure about your faith (which is an oxymoron in and of itself), explore them all. Without much effort, you will recognize that it only takes a day or two to dispatch the ridiculous ones. I am merely a layman in the realm of theology, but you do not need to split atoms to discern between what has been revealed and what is pure fallacy; it only takes time.

Part 3: Eventually We All Run Out of Cash

Money can be a nightmare; I know this from personal experience because I have made a ton of it in my lifetime and I've spent a ton too. You do the math. I never really wanted more out of life than to be comfortable, and although I will admit that there have been times when I have fantasized about becoming rich, I've never been too obsessed with the idea. What I have always wanted, however, was freedom from the worry that money brings, though in recent years that has changed. I still want freedom, but for completely different reasons and in a new way. Today, I simply have a desire to tell people what truth is about and the freedom that is contained in the knowledge of that truth. So when friends and family tell me that all they want out of life is to have enough money to take care of their family and retire comfortably, it makes me wonder. What about post-retirement? Are we so removed from a faith-based society that we can't even ask these kinds of questions?

One of my lifelong friends excels in the game of life better than most, and it would appear to most that he seems to have it made. In every way imaginable, he earned it. He has worked diligently for twenty-two years and has always been focused on what needed to be done. He is a great friend, an honest man, and basically a pillar in his extended family. I can talk to him about anything in the world, as long as the conversation never actually leaves the world.

This particular friend, like most kids growing up in Ojai, was raised a Christian. In fact, I remember praying out loud for the first time at his house when I was about six. His mom and dad seemed very devout in their belief and sincerely wanted to pass their faith down to their children. My friend always followed the rules and seemed to really like his family faith, but somewhere along the way, he may have put God in the back seat. He earned his degree and quickly went to work for a multimillion-dollar firm and never looked back. Now, firmly in his forties, he is as generous as they come—trustworthy, humorous, and pretty much loved by everyone who knows him. So why is it so hard to talk to him about matters of faith? When I thought I knew everything about theology, though sadly mistaken, I had no problem filling the air with blather. Now that I feel that I have stumbled onto some solid truths, I find myself steering clear of such conversations. It may be the fact that I make it clear with no uncertainties that my faith is now what encompasses me and therefore I have developed a slight fear of being ridiculed by those who do not share my world view. It's much easier to be a half-hearted Christian, simply because you will be deemed as less threatening.

On the flip side of the equation, I now feel convicted to my faith, and while I have a desire to be taken more seriously, I have long since realized that people do not like to be preached to, especially by one of their peers. It is one thing to express how you feel or even what you believe, but to say you actually know something to be true is to imply that someone with an opposing idea is wrong, and that is seen as rude and unwanted. My friend claims to be a Christian, but he doesn't want to talk about Christianity. His wife claims to believe in a God, but that her God could never be as judgmental and cruel as to sentence people to hell. I remember laughing at the term "her God," as if she created the Creator to fit her specifications. Those comments were made twenty years ago (when we were both young and naive), and it should be noted that my friend's wife has always been one of the most gracious people to have ever entered my life, and she has influenced me in many wonderful ways.

Amazingly, that pick-and-choose mentality of creating your own faith is commonplace these days. I've known this particular friend for thirty-nine years, and I still have no idea what he really believes or what his world view actually contains. His heart may be in good order, but I truly have no idea. I recently asked him about his future, and he didn't get any further than his desire to secure his family and retire comfortably. Hopefully he will fulfill his hardwired desire to know more about our existence, as it will surely add to his already quality character. We all have so much to learn.

I will never pretend to know what is in another's heart. I will, however, use logic, reason, and my own personal experience to make certain assumptions. Before you form a mob to track me down and burn me at the stake, keep in mind that everybody does this, as it is in our nature to judge. When you can openly admit your evil deeds and thoughts, then you can truly help other people with their struggles. Placing yourself in the same boat permits the helping of others to be deemed as less threatening and will become an awesome and powerful tool to possess.

I have spent countless hours lying in bed, thinking about the people in my life. Why does it seem as if so many people simply neglect God? There are many reasons for neglecting God, but primarily it comes down to courting the lures of life. Obviously, we have been infiltrated with a "me-first" attitude that has sprung up from postmodern thought, and these shallow virtues are depicted as the "good life" in ads and entertainment, while everybody seeks their personal slice of the pie. People will go to great lengths to get what they desire, and there is footage complete with surround sound to entice the buyer every step of the way. It has always amazed me that we live in a free country where we can obtain all the existing knowledge that has ever been written, and yet for so many, the quest for knowledge is lost in lieu of the next barbecue or the gains in their 401k.

Just a Thought #3

Not long ago, an American businessman had what most would consider a wonderful and successful life. He had a lucrative career, a big house, a beautiful wife, and the whole nine yards. He sold his business and his house and left for a foreign country to spread the word of God and help others. When his friends told him he was crazy to give up everything he had worked for, he simply replied, "One is never crazy to give up what he could never keep to gain that which he could never lose."

Chapter 5

The "Secret" Revealed

Part 1: Please Check Your Ego at the Door

I have a friend who is a Buddhist. At least he was the last time I asked. Between the two of us, there is a lot of animosity about theology. He was raised a Mormon and believes that Mormonism is traditional Christianity, and though I could go on and on about the stark and contrasting difference between the two, that will remain for another chapter. He had made the statement that Christianity was silly about fifty times prior to our final discussion on these matters. On a particularly long road trip, the topic of God came to the forefront, and we hadn't driven ten miles from my house before the conversation turned ugly. We bantered back and forth about origins and destiny and basically disagreed about everything metaphysical. He had a naturalistic explanation for our existence and believed that we create our own future. I believe the opposite. The conversation heated when he described Christianity as "unbelievably egotistical" and that the main tenet of Buddhism is letting go of ego. Well, obviously I couldn't let that go, because I believe the opposite to be true.

Buddhism puts everything into the hands of the individual, who is merely awake. You're in the driver's seat, and you are in control of your own destiny. How well you behave determines your next existence. In other words, it is all about the individual, and that equates to an egotistical ideology, though cleverly disguised with inner humility. Christianity claims that all are born into sin and are dependent on a Savior to deliver us from that sin. We must admit we are powerless and admit our wrongs, then seek forgiveness that is unmerited. Everything a Christian receives in the next life is undeserved and cannot be earned. Pride and ego do not now, nor have they ever, lent a hand in Christianity.

Eastern philosophy comes in many forms. It has been packaged and repackaged so many times in the West that it is hard to keep up. There are clever words and catch phrases that these peddlers use to lure their listeners. Words like *aura* and *energy* seem to have a hypnotic effect on the unsuspecting buyer. What you won't hear are words like *ontology, epistemology, deity, foundationalism, apologetics, sovereignty, trinity, incarnation,* and *resurrection,* because these are the kind of words that require reading and study. Books based in mystical thought are self-contained. They quickly and fluently depict the idea that their pages contain all you will ever need to know about everything, in and out of our perceived existence. The public continues to buy these books and tapes by the millions in a futile attempt to satisfy their inner thought process. At least it is good to know that there are people out there who still desire some form of an answer. A good question to ask when you find yourself reading about a mystical philosophy is this: "Could it really be this simple?"

As I stated before, there are countless books with inspiring words of blather that simplify our existence. They are similar in content, and although each new theory mysteriously changes the wording, they rarely venture far from the original tree. Hinduism and Buddhism are more complex than these new watered-down versions, but not by much. I have read many of these books, and the general theme never seems to alter; knowledge of this fact is a good foundation to build from. I vowed to never buy another mystical book again, but when a particular book takes the nation by a storm, I needed to see what all the fuss was about.

Part 2: Secretly Secretive

The Secret by Rhonda Byrne is the latest—and by sheer numbers one of the greatest-selling pieces of drivel that has come down the pipe in a long time. The book uses simple terms that are repeated time and again from people who have discovered "The Secret." These contributors are more than willing to share the secret with "You" for about twenty-five dollars. I capitalized the word "you" on purpose, to illustrate the first point Byrne makes in her introduction. She tells the reader that she will capitalize the "Y" in the book whenever she writes the word "you" because she wants the reader to know that it is all about YOU. Sound familiar? The word *universe* is used on countless occasions because the universe is your best friend that will give you everything that your heart desires. I can illustrate everything that you need to know about the book in six quick points, and if you understand these points, you can save your twenty-five bucks and live happily ever after.

Point #1: The secret is the law of attraction. It is perfect.
Point #2: Your thoughts attract like thoughts.
Point #3: Your thoughts are the finest and most powerful transmitters in the whole universe.
Point #4: Whatever you desire, think good things about it, believe and receive.
Point #5: Pretend you already have received what it is you desire, because time happens simultaneously, therefore you already have.
Point #6: With knowledge of the secret, the universe will re-align itself for you and manifest your every desire.

You're welcome, and if you feel a little guilty, you can send *me* your twenty-five dollars and I'll give it to a worthwhile charity. This book contains absolutely nothing new and yet blathers on and on about the preceding six points until the reader is nauseous. It does contain a few crazy ideas that branch out on their own, and I would be out of character to not share some of the more outlandish ones. Besides, I want to earn the twenty-five dollars, and you want you to get your money's worth. There is a story contained in the tiny two-hundred-page book (that would only have about fifty pages if it were normal size) that says it all. One person tried to trick the infallible law of attraction by imagining a feather that only existed in his mind. He made his image of the feather unique with certain markings and he then applied the points that I described earlier, and apparently the universe flopped the exact feather at his feet in New York City. Voila! It's that easy. Oh, and by the way, eat whatever you want and walk through Harlem at night with a boom box playing Barry Manilow at full volume, because if you truly believe that you will remain at the perfect weight and that you will never be murdered, the universe will take care of those requests too. This book is completely and utterly ridiculous, and I can punch many holes through the theory in my sleep.

First Blow:

Imagine that four people responsible for writing this book want the same thing. We'll use their first names, Bob, Joe, Marci, and of course Rhonda herself; contributors all. A problem arises in the universe because Bob, Joe, Marci, and Rhonda are all approximately the same age, and they all want a particular painting. They all share the desire to keep this painting in their family and pass it down from generation to generation. But this is not just any painting; it is a particular Rembrandt and it currently resides on the wall of a very rich man's house. He is selling the painting; so therefore, Bob, Joe, Marci, and Rhonda all have reason to believe that they can obtain it. The problem is that they all know the secret and the secret is perfect. So how will the universe solve the dilemma? We cannot obtain *everything* we desire if formulated into our "everything" is a one-of-a-kind item that another "secret" bearer wants at the same time.

Second Blow:

The book mentions mass fatalities, and while it doesn't delve too deeply into specifics regarding these fatalities, it probes the idea with an obvious premonition that the question will arise. Go figure. The book simply states that although the people who died simultaneously might not have had the exact thoughts, they must have had similar negative thoughts. I guess they want us to believe that every person who died in the Nazi death camps and the Soviet Gulags was inadvertently having bad thoughts. There couldn't have been a single person who held their head high and had faith that they would be delivered from captivity. Remember, the secret is perfect. What about the children and babies who died in these travesties? Many of the Jewish children actually believed that they were going to get candy in those chambers. According to Byrne and her ilk, nobody ever died in a car accident who didn't believe that they were going to. You can avoid anything bad and receive all that is good by transmitting positive thoughts, without exception. The only catch is that you need to pretend that you have already received it. In fact, you can't even think about how to obtain something you desire, because your attempts to form a plan will upset the universe with doubting thoughts and hence keep the *feather* hidden.

Final Blow:

This absurdity is stolen and repackaged from age-old writings. It is nothing new and should be disregarded without impunity. Obviously, there are a lot of people who take this book seriously, based on the fact that it has sold millions and has become an overnight American sensation. Ironically, in the few years that this book has been purchased by the masses and handed to countless more, our country has seen a decline in everything good. Greed and corruption have run wild, and the economy is currently on a resuscitator. Is it possible that all these people who have learned the secret could be using it to destroy our very way of life? Maybe the knowledge of the secret is in the wrong hands of the greedy, or possibly too many of them simply want the same thing, mainly cash. That would explain why we are printing money faster than ever before and why we have halted the production of goods to back it up. I guess the universe needs it to manifest large sums of money for all of the new masters who are living this new lavish lifestyle with zero need to be productive. Maybe that's why the rest of us are so broke, darn! Secret people! If there numbers are growing, and by all accounts they are, then the secret knower's must not be sending the right thoughts from their "greatest transmitters in the universe," because things are not going well since this book came into print.

The Secret is once again on the bestseller list, and personally I think it is in the wrong category. To call this book nonfiction is the equivalent of depicting Cher as the next Mother Teresa.

If you are inclined to read these types of books, then ask yourself a couple of questions: How many times before have I been intrigued by this sort of mystical idealism? How many ideas that are contained in the book that I'm currently reading were borrowed from books that I have already read? You might find that you've been aimlessly running in circles. It will require some honesty, but you eventually develop the humility required to discard these simpler explanations to our existence. In the long run, you will have no choice.

To summarize, there is a line drawn between Eastern and Western thought, and whether you like it or not, you have a world view that most likely falls into one of these two camps. You might believe that the universe is all there is, and that you have complete control over it and everything else. You might believe that the universe is all there is, and that you have absolutely zero control over it, but remain in complete control over yourself and your personal destiny. Both of these world views are deeply entrenched in Eastern thought.

On the opposite side of the fence, you might believe that the universe is not all there is. Believing that there is something or somebody beyond the universe leaves you no choice but to believe in a Creator. Do the math. If there is a Creator and you believe that he is not personally involved, then it is still possible to imagine yourself in the driver's seat. A problem may arise, however, when you realize that the car has no engine, and try as you might, you won't get very far beyond the grave. Finally, suppose you believe that the universe is not all there is and that you do believe in a Creator who is personally involved. This is the simplest form of Western thought. This line of thinking, defiantly through humility, puts us in the back seat. The biggest problem with Western thought is that our pride doesn't like the back seat, so we tend to deny our own beliefs for the less-restricting ones. Although easy to read and understand, *The Secret* has very little to offer in reality.

Chapter 6

"The Wayward West"

Part 1: We Want to Believe
(in just about anything)

Studying church history is a long process, and I will be quick to admit that I'm by no means an expert. I do enjoy learning about the origins and traditions of different denominations of Christianity, and I have been intrigued with spin-offs from the original as well. Islam and Mormonism are two of the bigger spin-offs from the biblical account. I have problems with both, and I will explain my concerns in more detail at another point, but for now, it can be summed up in one word: "man." Every time man adds his own ideas to that of the Creator and calls it holy, we have a problem brewing. People have long had an infatuation with man-made ideologies, because they offer simple solutions that come from people just like them. This infatuation seems to fill the void to their longing for answers without the toiling of inquiry. So many are easily intrigued by the outrageous claims of their fellow man and use these fallacies to justify their means. Moving away from the comfort zone provided in these simple explanations is like removing the training wheels off the bicycle of a two-year-old; we know a fall is imminent. We may fall and scrape our knees, we might even break an arm or lose a tooth, but I'd rather have the scars of being right than a seventy-year-old rolling down the street on a bicycle with four wheels.

It is easy to dismiss all religion as a crutch for the weak of mind, but unfortunately for the skeptic, history proves otherwise. Academic skeptics are revered in the classrooms and lecture halls but rarely make appearances on the battlefield of real-life matters. These scholarly skeptics will be quick to denounce religion as a fabrication to control the masses or a delusion to satisfy the wandering mind, but when called to action, these "knower's of all" will usually hide behind their lecterns of rights.

God-fearing men braved our shores centuries ago, while skeptical Europeans read books of enlightenment in finely crafted mahogany libraries. God-fearing men wrote our Declaration of Independence and our Constitution, while skeptical elitists set up camp in our classrooms and public squares. God-fearing men built our infrastructure and defended our nation, while skeptics protested our innovation and denounced our military might. God-fearing men raised their children to believe in a higher power and the virtues that come from above, while skeptics—who generally have fewer children—remained in waiting to abolish said beliefs and virtues when left alone with our children. God-fearing writers speak in terms of love, devotion, and honor, while skeptical writers speak in terms of hatred of religion and dissent toward all that is good.

History contains an abrupt answer to the underlying question in regards to religious attributes of American society. God-fearing men, for the most part, designed and developed our nation from the ground floor and protected its sovereignty, while the enlightened skeptics have been dreaming and scheming how to destroy it from within.

Part 2: Da Vinci Decoded

Another bestseller based on erroneous information is *The Da Vinci Code,* which is admittedly fiction but with an asterisk. The author, Dan Brown, claims that he began working on the project in hopes that he would disprove his hypothesis, when suddenly he began to believe it. Luckily, when I was about eight, I used logic and reason to determine that I wasn't really Batman, but that's another story altogether. Apparently, these skills of logic and reason that I learned so early in life are lost on Mr. Brown. The story is remotely entertaining, as it evokes a bizarre look into history and submits some hilarious conclusions. It is also quite offensive to believers and requires a rebuttal based in reason.

The Da Vinci Code is based on an idea that there were several purposely omitted gospels left out of the final Bible as we know it today. Brown claims that Constantine chose which books would be included in the Bible and which ones were to be left out, to secure the divinity of Jesus. The omitted books devalue Jesus as a deity and promote him as a completely different character; thus Constantine, being a Christian by all accounts, wasn't going to allow any of that. Brown then reaches so far as to promote Mary Magdalene as the wife of Jesus, the mother of his offspring, and the main rock on which his church will be built. Keep in mind that Brown claims to believe this. What I believe is that Brown is either really stupid, delusional, or wants to make money. You choose $$. History quickly and simply answers the false claims found in the novel.

First we need to determine when the existing gospels were written. In a liberal dating scale, the four gospels were written between AD 50 and 100. And since Jesus died in AD 33, they were written shortly after the events occurred.

Blow #1

Most Gnostic (esoteric thought) or so-called *gospels* were not left out by Constantine. The matter had been closed a century and a half before his Council. Look it up.

Blow #2

Gnosticism was considered a cult by early Christians, mainly because they were written 100 to 400 years after the events themselves. They were secret in their nature and were counter-intuitive to the original gospels. Basically they made no sense to early Christians and were therefore disregarded.

Blow #3

Why do they call the bloodline of Jesus the Holy Grail when the bloodline of a mere mortal is not holy? Think about it!

Blow #4

The Priory of Sion was a hoax made up in 1956 by a Frenchman. Without these guys, the book loses all validity. There is no Da Vinci and Newton protecting the Grail in a priory that never existed.

Blow #5

The Knights Templar existed, but Brown claims that they were formed by the non-existing Priory to protect a secret which hundreds of years before had been disregarded.

Final Blow:

Dan Brown knows that his book is complete blather and should be taken as such. He could have hidden behind the fictional shield forever if he hadn't committed himself to the belief that Jesus was married with children. Al Bundy, Jesus Christ; I can't tell the difference. Sadly, many believe these bizarre claims because they never take the five minutes required to research the historical falsehoods blanketing Brown's novel. The pop culture has a strong desire for easy answers, and guys like Brown give it to them, for about thirty dollars a pop. Brown realizes that it is much more profitable to indulge the believer than to admit the shortcomings of his hypothesis. By the way, on a side note, Tom Hanks, while taking a role in the film version of the novel, should be ashamed of himself. He'll claim that it is a fictional character, but deep down he knows that a lot of people buy the whole enchilada, and that makes him a contributor to the lie.

Part 3: Choices

Here in America, we love to choose. Choice has become the greatest of virtues; it even trumps the choices we make. Abortion, anyone?

Abortion makes me wince, and I like to think that it makes most people wince, but I guess we all have the choice to deny it. Regardless of the circumstances, we are punishing the wrong person, and then we look for a reason that is not a matter of convenience. One doesn't exist. Movies on demand are a cool feature, but abortion on demand makes blood shoot out of my eyes. Freedom of choice is given to us by the Deity, but today we want to believe that there are no consequences to our choices. Deep down, we know that is not the case; it is merely a false hope that we choose to believe. We are in a constant state of making laws, and yet we rarely abolish any, but if our choices were evolving in the right direction, the opposite would be true. Maybe, just maybe, if we made better choices, we could put some legislators on a bus back to their homes, where many belong.

We are bombarded with choices, and if we are having trouble making up our minds, we simply mix and match and form new concoctions until we find a sense of satisfaction. We have become the new proprietors of our very own existence, where the virtue of choice is seen as more prudent than the complexities of understanding God.

Do we really want a God who gives us authority over his personal existence? You do realize that to believe this, you are essentially saying that you are God. At the very least, you make up a portion of the truth that is God. Either way, you are taking away his sovereignty and putting your fate into your own hands or the collective hands of everybody else. For some, God is not separate from creation, God *is* the creation. The doors that open up here are infinite. With this derailed line of thinking, you can make up a personal philosophy that suits your every inclination. Take a tidbit of Hinduism and Native American thought and sprinkle it with some Roman Catholicism, and you will have created a new and improved faith that is tailor-made to fit your very existence. A serious problem may arise when we come to understand that words actually have meanings, and like it or not, they dictate our logic.

If you see a red truck run over a puppy at the same time and place in which I saw a blue Yugo run over that same puppy, one of us is going to be wrong, unless we excuse truth altogether, but that requires a PhD in logic. Holy books don't agree on much when you get down to their core meaning. They need to be gutted of their sole purpose in order to make them fit as one, and this gutting has begun. Choosing what remnants of each faith to believe and discarding the remainder is about as logical as towing your car to the car wash and neglecting the fact that it doesn't have an engine. It is a choice to do irrational things, but unfortunately for some, we don't choose God. He, in fact, chooses us. We don't choose right and wrong, we simply perform deeds, whether good or bad. Our destiny is our only real choice that has any relevance, and we'll touch on that later.

In most situations that we are faced with while being human, we generally know what we ought to do. I suppose it is possible to have a heart so blackened that you no longer have a moral compass, but if so, you're probably in no mood to be reading this anyway. Choice is a gift, and if used correctly, it can be an awesome thing. Unfortunately, humans are flawed and we seem to make bad choices time and again. Adam made a bad choice, and he knew it to be a bad choice firsthand. Cain made the wrong choice to slay Abel, and it gets worse from there. When faced with a choice, we have three possible outcomes: we either do what we ought to do, what we want to do, or what we instinctively do.

We ought to save the girl in distress, but we want to keep ourselves safe. We ought to stay away from adultery, but we want to have a moment of bliss. The real culprit is when we think that we can have both, but that abolishes the very meaning of the word "choice." Remember, words still mean things, at least for the time being. Moral choices have led to the rise of excuses. "Ought" becomes "would" in a hurry. I would have saved the girl if didn't have an important presentation to make. I would have remained faithful to my wife if she didn't complain so much. Any excuse will do. People have a morality outside of our basic instincts that sets us apart from other animals and this sense of morality is currently being ignored by way too many.

Some sense of right and wrong is learned in our upbringing, but overall we know when we do something wrong because it makes us feel bad. If the argument is to be made that all morality is learned, then we must ask from whom. If all we know about right and wrong is learned then who decided what was right and wrong in the first place. People who deny God would lead you to believe that we evolved to a point of knowing and we are still on the highway to learning more. We make new laws, just to keep pace, whenever a group of people decide to invent new ways to cheat or abuse. Regardless of how new the misdeed is, the people who commit the misdeeds knew they were wrong before they acted. Jeffrey Dahmer might have been sick, but he knew that steering clear of Bumble Bee tuna fish for an off-beat brand was probably not a good idea. If all morality is learned, then who taught the first man? Did we have a particular day in our evolution where suddenly chopping off a cat's tail went from good behavior to bad? Or did we start by chopping off smaller pieces?

Humans have a little thing called a conscience, and it is the infallible meter in our brains that never lies. Basically, if you feel bad about something you did, then you probably shouldn't have done it. Others will try to ease your guilt because they are trying to erase their own, and we have all been guilty of this at one time or another. If we spent even a fraction of our time seeking the originator of morality, as we do trying to erase our conscience, we would become a much richer people. Our conscience can save us from our unpleasant deeds at the moment of choice, but after that moment has come and gone, we are left with either a sense of calm or guilt. Both of these sensations are hard-wired from the start of our existence, and they are a tremendous gift.

When we weigh our indiscretions against others, it is possible to find some sense of peace. If my neighbor is a drunkard and beats his wife, then by comparison, fudging on my taxes does not seem so bad. True peace however, will never be found until we weigh our indiscretions against God and truly see how far we have fallen. This will hopefully lead to admitting our wrongs and showing true sorrow. If we can expect a human judge who is far from perfect to implement harsh punishments to those who show little or no remorse for a single act of indiscretion, then how can we expect a perfect judge to forgive a lifetime of wrongs without true repentance?

Literary Critic Robert Langbaum once asserted on the condition of European thought, that there is no accepted morality or truth and that most of Europe is left with only vague perspectives of the matter. Are we expected to follow in the footsteps of our European neighbors and live a life of immorality or do we return to our traditional thought process that led to our prosperity

---

Just a Thought #4

Choice in sexual orientation can be a heated argument. The very fact that God has declared homosexuality an abomination is lost on many, including some men of the cloth. Putting aside the fact that most homosexuals are not God-fearing individuals, it should be noted that most are naturalists. If naturalism is true, then it must be conceded that survival of the fittest is true as well. If survival of the fittest is true, then how do we explain an increase of homosexuality? It should be apparent that in being unable to reproduce more of the same with similar genetic makeup, the numbers of homosexuals should be in a constant state of decline. Naturalism without choice eliminates homosexuals. Without relying on sexual orientation being a moral choice, the homosexual's days are numbered.

Part 4: The Eraser

Without God, there is no virtue, because there is no prompting of the conscience. Without God we're mired in the material, that flat world that tells us only what our senses perceive.

Ronald Reagan

When I was a kid, I loved magicians, and I truly thought they were performing miracles. When I learned they were fooling me with illusions, I lost all interest. My dad had little patience when it came to illusions as well, and fooling him was never a good idea. I remember back in my twenties I used modern technology to fool my parents and I've felt a tad guilty ever since. My sister had moved to a secluded ranch in upper Ojai, and she found herself a little afraid to be alone with her two small children when my brother-in-law was away for his two-day shifts at the fire department. I would, on occasion, spend the night there and keep them company. Satellite dishes were rare at the time, but since no cable was available at the ranch, my sister had one. I didn't know much about the programming schedule, but it didn't take long to realize that she received programs on the Eastern Time zone.

One day my sister and I were watching *Wheel of Fortune* at 4:30 in the afternoon when my mom called and asked me if I wanted to have dinner. At the time, I never thought of the trickery that I would pull later that night on my parents. My parents were trusting of their children, and they had no clue that I had the answers to the puzzles on that night's *Wheel of Fortune*. After dinner, we were playing a game of gin when I heard the show starting in the background, and as I was about to confess that I had already seen the episode, my plan was realized. I answered the puzzles with just enough revealed letters to make it believable. My mom was amazed with my newfound intellect, but my dad just gave me weird looks. I did this on a few separate occasions, but eventually I had to stop because my dad knew something was afoot and he wouldn't have been happy to know that I was fooling him. He wanted to say I was cheating on more than one occasion, but for the life of him, he couldn't figure out how. He simply gave me that intense glare of knowing, and I figured it was a good time to stop. To this day, my mom probably thinks that she raised a genius and probably wishes that I had made my way to the set for untold riches. My dad passed away several years back, and although I never told him, he knew the score.

Basically, we all have a general feeling that we are being fooled when the improbable is presented before us. The Bible contains many concepts that are hard to believe, but God is not trying to fool us. God merely dwells in dimensions that are beyond our understanding. With an extra dimension, we could walk through walls, but to God who dwells in multiple dimensions, that is mere child's play. If we lose a dimension, we are living in Flat Stanley world, where stumbling upon a round rock would appear to be a miracle.

I remember seeing a movie with Nicolas Cage called *The Family Man.* Cage plays a man who thinks he has it made. He is an executive living in New York City who is rich and powerful, and he enjoys all that life has to offer: women, cars, a giant flat in a prestigious part of Manhattan, and the list goes on. He is then shown a glimpse of what his life would have been like if he had chosen to stay with his girlfriend rather than leave her for a period abroad. It is a cute story, and of course it presents a moral at the end. I am however, more intrigued by a character in the film played by Don Cheadle. Cheadle is the giver of the glimpse and the provider for the moral. Oddly, they never say who he is; maybe he was an angel or something, but they never disclose his identity. Cheadle appears and disappears in odd locations when he is least expected. At one point in the film, he appears as a store clerk working the register where a young girl hands him a dollar for a candy bar, and he purposely gives her change for a ten. When she leaves, he looks at Cage and says with disgust, "Man, and for nine dollars and change." The young girl felt guilt, it showed on her face, but she took the money anyway. The question that comes to mind is this: Will she always feel the same level of guilt? Does guilt erode? Are we solely responsible for the erosion of guilt or can society play a role?

Everybody wants to erase the feeling of guilt, and we all have an ally in our attempts: society. We are being infiltrated with the idea that guilt is not good for us. It's not your fault, society created your behavior, and therefore there is no reason to sweat about it. If it feels good, then do it, unless of course it upsets somebody else or it doesn't fit tightly into the politically correct. Getting drunk can be considered humorous and endearing simply because it is legal. Getting drunk and hitting your wife is still considered wrong. Smoking pot is considered wrong by most, simply because it is not legal. Many people feel little or no guilt when drinking in excess, as long as they don't cause any problems, but if the substance of choice is illegal, people generally feel more guilt.

Society, (to a degree) sets the level of guilt by marketing one substance as worse than the other. Just because society allows for a particular behavior to be deemed as okay while another is not doesn't make either right. It is possible to have a drink or possibly two and keep complete control of your faculties, but when you exceed that level, you are compromising your ability to communicate with others, and more importantly, your ability to communicate with God. Smoking cigarettes is really bad for you, but it doesn't hinder your ability to communicate. Drinking sodas and eating cheeseburgers is really bad for you too, but that behavior doesn't hinder communication either. Other than the annoying smell, why is one so frowned upon while the other is accepted as okay? Who makes the rules? I have had a battle with cigarettes, and I wish that we lived in a smoke-free world, but a case can be made that communicating with God is a whole lot easier with damaged lungs than a damaged mind.

Any mind-altering drug, including alcohol, will bring irrational thoughts to the forefront. God probably doesn't want to talk to irrational train wrecks that are purposely in that state. God gave most of us clear minds for the sole purpose of seeking him. When segments of society try to dictate right from wrong, it is usually an attempt to eliminate their own guilt. There are proponents of legalizing drugs of every kind, and amazingly, there are also proponents of legalizing man-boy love affairs. The list goes on and on, and where it stops is anybody's guess. People who lobby for these ideas may not be drug users or pedophiles themselves, but they probably have something to else to hide. Making particularly despicable acts legal makes the lesser displeasing acts more acceptable, and the more that act is accepted, the less guilt one feels about committing the act. Every time we turn a blind eye to these proponents of illogical changes in the law, society suffers the consequence.

Only the Creator can erase our guilt, because he gave it to us in the first place. Nothing that exists can be put out of existence by man. I don't want to get too deep into physics, but we can only move matter around, and we currently do not have the ability to take anything out of existence. Guilt is even harder to remove, because it doesn't swim in the physical realm. It is a feeling, and try as you may, neither you nor society can destroy it. Embrace guilt as a compass and use your compass to behave correctly. Once in a while, remember to thank God that you have guilt.

Just a Thought #5

When playing baseball, a batter might have a second or two to decide whether to swing at a fastball or not. To say the least, he is focused. When you are faced with a tough decision that doesn't require a sudden response, the emotional reaction is not always the correct one. Christians use prayer to seek the wisdom of God to make the right decision. Eastern philosophy uses meditation to be enlightened to the right choice. If you believe in God and place your full trust in him, then you can trust that what he is telling you to do is correct. The answer might not be what you want, and the results might seem wrong in every way, but that doesn't make the decision wrong in God's eyes. True faith requires a trust that God has a will for all things to work toward his purpose. Knowledge that God has a perfect will can help you find a level of peace in your decisions.

Chapter 7

Fame and Fortune

Part 1: Celebrities Gone Wild

J.R.R. Tolkien was a brilliant writer. Very few have possessed the imagination that he so eloquently put into words. Tolkien also had an understanding of idolatry and the destruction that it can bring into our lives. In the final book in the *Lord of the Rings* series, we find our hero Frodo battling his morality between doing what is right and the inner idolatry of the ring and its power:

At the climax of the story Frodo struggles between the two powers encompassing him. He held a deep desire to keep the ring but in the end he came to his better senses and took it off and freed himself of eventual destruction.

Frodo chose wisely. He set aside his earthly desires and the treasures that only the ring could grant, for something far better. Celebrities have a lot of rings. When the time comes will they be willing to place them on the altar or will they grasp hard to the glitter and the gold?

If you care about who's sleeping with Madonna or what low-cut dress J-Lo wore to the Oscars, then you're probably reading the wrong book. You can find your book at the checkout stand. I find it humorous that Sean thinks he's an intellectual and that Jennifer still loves Brad, but I can't find myself caring or even remotely interested. If you wish to delve into the crazy and absurd ideas coming from these Hollywood elites, then you can easily find countless books documenting them. I'm much more interested in why they think the way they do. I realize that every person is different, but when a large group of people act and react in a similar fashion that is completely separate from the normal society in which they came, there has to be a reason behind it. Some—but not many—have tried to explain this phenomenon, and though I may be far removed from the fray, I have some theories. Contained in these ideas are many truths, but in the end, my conclusions will remain "just in theory."

Imagine that you are either extremely talented or, as Ben Stiller says in *Zoolander,* "really, really good-looking." Then imagine that you are paid large sums of money to perform those talents or stand around looking good. Finally, imagine everybody you know is constantly telling you how great you are. Whether your inner circle likes you or not, they will love the fringe benefits that come along with knowing you. If Britney acts like a spoiled idiot, then somebody close to her ought to say, "Britney, you're acting like a spoiled idiot," but then who would pay for the new Escalade? Celebrities are surrounded by "yes men" who will cater to their ego at every turn. They will be their first line of defense when something goes wrong. "Winona didn't mean to steal; she was just so exhausted from feeding the homeless and under such tremendous pressure to fund her youth foundation that she momentarily lost track of who she was." By the way, have you seen my new Escalade? If you treat somebody like a god long enough, they will begin to believe it. God, by nature, doesn't do well with sharing the spotlight with other gods, and that explains why you need to buy a lot of groceries to be informed on the latest Hollywood rumors perpetrated by those who in some twisted way believe that they are gods.

Contrary to what some might think, most celebrities were raised relatively normal. If the transformation starts too soon or if they are born into stardom, you get Danny Bonaduce or Liza Minelli. In Hollywood, I suppose it is possible to get a cross between the two, but that's for another writer. Most celebrities start out learning true-blue American values and are then bombarded with non-traditional ideology at the gates of stardom. This is eerily similar to what happens to our children when we drop them off at the hallowed grounds of a higher learning institute. The difference between a college-bound kid and the bound-for-glory kid is that the potential star already thinks they are something extraordinary. If an individual already thinks that they stand above the norm, then convicting them to that idea is that much easier. Not all famous people want to be famous, and it is interesting that those particular celebrities seem to be the most wholesome and humble.

Part 2: American Idolatry

Worshipping anything but the one true God is a form of idolatry. In many cases, it is a material item, but for most it is merely themselves. Never before has this form of self-idolatry been on public display in the way that it is currently being portrayed on *American Idol*. I will always give credit where credit is due, and the creators of the show are at least honest in the title. I would have taken it a step further and called the show "American Self-Idolatry," but that might not have resonated well with the viewers.

The show is fun to watch and can be very entertaining. I personally love quality music, and it can, on occasion, be found on this program. There is nothing inherently wrong with having a gifted voice and wanting to share it with the world. However, when we neglect the fact that your beautiful voice is a gift, idolatry grabs you with its slimy fingers, and sadly, this is the case for most of these young contestants. Their friends and family do not offer much in the way of perspective while worshipping them and placing them on a pedestal while dollar signs roll in their eyes. Wanting fame and fortune is appealing to everyone to a degree, and we all want to play the hero at some point in our lives, because we see the accolades that come along with it and we desire them. Who wouldn't want admiration and an abundance of earthly goods for singing, dancing, or pretending? It is only when you see the possible disconnect from God and the realm of eternity that these ideas of fame subside. A side of me wants this book to do well, and I would be lying if I said that I didn't want the approval of others that I did a good job. However, if I thought for one second that this book could separate me from God, then I would be on my way to Staples to buy a paper shredder.

There is a huge problem in the human soul when we see ourselves as something more special than others simply because we have a unique talent. Here's a news flash: everybody is talented; finding your talent is the real chore at hand. If your particular talent is pleasing to watch or hear, then the masses will pay to see or hear your talent. The fact that others will pay for your talents doesn't make you better than anyone else, and certainly no more enlightened. You just have an admired talent. Good for you; now shut up and sing! If you are placed on a pedestal because of a particular talent, then it is up to you to realize that you actually are no more deserving to be on that pedestal than a talented bricklayer. *American Idol* is a talent/popularity contest where American viewers choose whom to idolize. When the *American Idol* contestant is chosen to be the contest winner, that individual needs to keep a perspective contrasted by God and avoid the trap so cleverly set by those around them.

Putting perspective on a newfound celebrity status must be tough. It is not the blessing that it appears. The individual who lays bricks will have an easier chance of finding true perspective, simply because laying bricks from a pedestal is hard on the back. Having parents and friends adore you every step of the way during your rise to fame can't help much either. It truly sickens me when I see parents slobber over their children's talent, and this show is filled with tears. Parents cry when their child excels and they cry tears of discontentment when their child is sent home. I've yet to hear a parent tell his or her kid that they just weren't good enough and that maybe joining the military would be a good option. Supporting your kids in their endeavors is one thing, but lying to them when their talent obviously lies elsewhere is a shame. That is why the average viewer loves Simon Cowell. He seems to realize that some people are meant to lay bricks, and he's not afraid to say it. Cowell might not be a humble guy himself, but at least he knows that some people need to be. Once we realize that all of us are talented in our own right, we can shed the idolatry that comes from fame. If perspective is lost on a famous person, then the person will suffer the consequences of becoming laughable.

Most famous people have outrageous ideas that stem from their self-idolatry. They seem to either love or condone misguided behavior, and for some reason they generally detest anything traditional or Christian. They love their free speech and smear others with opposing thoughts. In their minds, it must appear as if they have obtained the best solutions to every problem and since they never hear anything contrary from those around them, what are they to think? When these celebrities make their non-sense known to the world and the world laughs at them; they are quickly surrounded by individuals who will assure them that it is the 99.999 percent of humanity that is sadly mistaken and that their ideas are surely enlightened.

In conclusion, my theory is this: celebrities think they are smarter and much more enlightened than the average individual, and they receive large sums of cash and constant pats on the back to re-affirm it. They are surrounded by scoundrels who will cater to their every wish to stay in good graces and lush hotels. They are led by others in their inner circle to believe that they are the chosen ones and it is their duty to offer their unique words of wisdom. Whatever crazy ideas they submit must be taken seriously by their ilk, and those ideas will be reflected back to the star as profound and insightful. They are talented and gifted at best, and in some cases just really, really good-looking. Not all celebrities fall into this trap, but most do. When you think about how lucky and blessed they are, remember, they are so far removed from reality that in many cases, finding God is reduced to channeling a Greek goddess through Shirley McLain or paying hundreds of thousands of dollars to jump around on couches like Tom Cruise.

Part 2: Imagine there's No Wisdom

Musicians have it so much easier than actors, because they do not need to rely solely on looks or weight scales to get a gig. Take Bob Dylan for instance. He is talented beyond belief, but he isn't going to win a beauty contest anytime soon. Musicians need to rely on talent, and although this talent can be electronically enhanced to make an average singer like Britney Spears sound great, when her looks and dance moves fail and she is left with only her voice to rely on, she probably won't be selling out the Staples Center at that point. Longevity in the music business seems to be set apart for those who really have musical talent, and through their microphones they can let the world know how they feel. Looking at just a few of these singer-songwriters, we can find some commonalities. Most feel that it is their duty to inform the world of our social injustices, and their songs are filled with jabs at the established system and our core traditional values.

Probably the most famous song in their cause is "Imagine" by John Lennon. The song was beautifully performed last year on *American Idol* by a young contestant named David Archuleta. When he finished the song, he received a standing ovation by all in attendance, and the three judges laced their comments with praise for the leftist songwriter himself. I found it interesting that a song which is so divisive can be labeled as the greatest ballad of all time. If you put aside your thoughts of nirvana for a moment and listen to what Lennon is trying to convey, the song quickly loses its luster.

Everybody wants peace. Even radical jihadists want peace. They believe that once they chop the heads off all non-believing infidels, they will live in peace. Lennon's idea of global peace is not a bad thing, but his disregard for logic and human nature makes his road map to peace hard to follow. World peace can only be achieved when the Creator is in charge and the human condition is reversed. John Lennon was not God. I realize that to some of his fans, he is considered a god, but talented melodies and rhyming words won't elevate you to divinity. Lennon, while led astray by many factors, was a true believer in peace. His only problem was that he believed that peace could manifest with man in charge. "Imagine" is a sacred cow to many, and breaking it down to pure hogwash is going to upset a lot of people. The sheer mention of the song and my finding it distasteful has probably already irritated some of you, so what do I have to lose?

#1 Lennon wants us to imagine an existence with no afterlife

Okay, so our current existence is all there is and together we can speed up evolution and live in pure harmony if we all just hold hands. This is never going to happen, and deep down we all know it.

#2 Lennon wants us to imagine that there are no eternal consequences.

Okay, so justice is out. *Do as thou wilt* is the new mantra, and I guess we will be transferred into a perfect society where people will just magically start doing the right thing even though they will have zero consequences if they don't. We make laws for many reasons, but doing the right thing isn't one of them.

#3 Lennon expects us to believe that there is nothing worth physically fighting for.

Okay, let's slap the faces of all those who have given their life to free millions from enslavement and to preserve a better way of life. It's probably best that we ignore those getting their heads chopped off or the people who at one time inhaled too much gas. There will always be evildoers and those willing to make the ultimate sacrifice to stop them.

#4 Lennon believes that we should abandon all religion.

This should be insulting to most people; 90 percent of people believe in some form of religion. Some will call their religion a philosophy, but make no mistake: it's a religion. Worshipping the ground you walk on is a religion, and if you are endeared to all of Earth's creatures in a fanatical way, then the world is your religion. Even atheists are religious in that they stake their world view on there not being a God. For some, religion is not sacred, but to a large portion of American society, it is. What about those people? Do they cherish this song as well? If your faith is important to you, why would you stand and cheer for a song that says that you should shed your beliefs for a non-achievable ideology? If you are a Christian, a Hindu, a Mormon, a Catholic, or a

Buddhist, then that song should offend you. If you are a Muslim, I'm sure it already does, based purely on the fact that it was written by an English infidel. Amazingly, here in the West, we love this song and it shows more about our lethargic attitudes in preserving our belief system than anything else.

#5 Lennon wants us to know that he is not alone in his ideology.

He's right. He's not the only one, and that's what scares me. The more people who stake their claim to this idealistic nirvana, the more our defenses are lowered. Evil men will continue their dastardly ways and kill whoever opposes them. Call me crazy, but I don't think that a song or a large group of hippies holding hands is going to stop them. Ironically, this idealism receives the least respect from evildoers because they perceive it as weak. Hippies would be the first in line for the role of the headless horseman in Washington Irving's "Sleepy Hollow" if our soldiers didn't protect them.

Throughout history, it has been the inaction of those who could have acted; the indifference of those who should have known better; the silence of the voice of justice when it mattered most; that has made it possible for evil to triumph.

Haile Selassie

John Lennon spent weeks in bed, protesting for peace, while basically doing nothing. I suppose if we all went to bed for a few weeks, we would have a period of peace, but eventually people are going to get up. Some of us will be refreshed and so well-rested that killing a few extra would be a breeze. Doing nothing is never an option, and living a lie that is perpetrated by a sacred ballad will doom generations to enslavement.

There are many brave soldiers who risk their lives every day to keep us safe. The same can be said of the soldiers who performed their duties in the '60s and '70s while John Lennon was taking his long nap. Nobody likes war, and although there are bad eggs in every basket, common sense says that we should support the good guys. No matter how long we rest in bed and hope for peace, the boogeyman is not going to morph into Gandhi.

Part 3: Why so Many Love Songs?

If a song steers clear of vulgarity and it is not written to promote a point, then it is most likely a love song. Listen to the radio for an hour and you will hear that the larger percentage of songs pertain to love in one way or another. They are eerily similar to Christian songs, except for the object of affection. These heart-filled songs are generally more pleasing to the ear simply because trying to tell someone how much you love them to the music of "Highway to Hell" is a difficult task. Why do people want to fill the air with silly love songs, as Paul McCartney writes in his '70s classic? Because people are looking for an eternal love and our fellow man cannot supply that kind of love. Humans will let you down time and again, and this letdown is chronicled every three minutes on radios across the nation. I realize that some people are rocks, but they are far from perfect, and when your time on Earth is over, God's love is all that will matter. Eternal love is what we seek, the kind that is hardwired to our very existence and which no mere mortal can fill. Hopelessly, we try to fill this void with other people, but our attempts are in vain. Love songs depict our vanity.

I am not a love guru, but I've been around long enough to figure out a few things. No matter how great your relationship is, even if you worship the ground your partner walks on, it has limitations. A great love will only get you so far and it would be wise to think of your significant other as a gift, because that is all they are. They can help you in all the endeavors the world lays at your feet and you can return the favor, but it takes divine intervention to know true love. I went through women at an alarming speed until I married at forty. Without the love of God that my wife and I share, our odds of remaining true to each other would be greatly decreased. She is the best person I know, but I could form a reason to seek out another. Obviously, it would be the mistake of my life, because she is irreplaceable, but I could somehow justify it. It is true that the divorce rate among Christians is similar to the general public, but that doesn't take into account the rate of true believers and the fact that Christians are more likely to marry in the first place. When we make a commitment to God in the form of marriage, then breaking that commitment becomes a little more distasteful.

A love song can be easily transferred to God and vice versa. Van Morrison is a Christian who wrote the song "Have I Told You Lately." It is played at countless weddings where you find the bride and groom staring deeply into each other's eyes. Oddly, it is a love song written to God, but that seems to be lost on some people. You can take most love songs and replace the object of affection with God, and it won't skip a beat. Why is that? Could it be that our true desire lies somewhere beyond the human touch? I think so. Whitney was wrong when she sang, "Learning to love yourself, it is the greatest love of all." In fact, I believe the opposite to be true. Learning the truth about yourself and loving God is the greatest love of all. The real crushing truth is that we are not deserving of love at all.

I once asked a non-believer if he loved his mother and he answered with a resounding "yes." I then told him that it is possible for him to love his archenemy a thousand times more than he loves his mother at some point in eternity. I honestly believe that to be true, assuming they end up sharing eternity in the same place. It is possible for someone to stay by your side for many years and give you all the love they can muster, but if it is never reciprocated, then eventually they will leave. They may not physically leave, but emotionally they'll be long gone. The same is true with God. He will love you all your life, but if you never love him back, then eventually he will leave you. If you learn to love God, suddenly loving others becomes a whole lot easier. When you really break it down, God isn't asking for much. All things come to an end, except that which is eternally good. God is eternally good, and we can share in his likeness and live forever. Sappy love songs can bring temporal comfort, but God can bring eternal peace.

Chapter 8

Communication Breakdown

Part 1: Modern Tech 101

Modern communication has a tremendous upside. We can view events as they are happening with a simple flick of a switch or a push of a button. We can instantly be in communication with another person, regardless of where they currently reside. Lately, it has become popular to communicate without speaking at all as chat rooms and cell phone texting are the latest craze. We live in a "now" society, and it gets a little smaller every day. I'll admit that I use my cell phone on occasion; it is tremendously convenient, but mostly I prefer it when it doesn't ring. Today, we even enlist the choice whether to answer the phone or not, because we know who's on the other end of the line with caller ID. All this technology can be useful, but there is a price to pay. Our ability to communicate in person is being eroded.

Listen to a couple of typical twenty-year-olds talk to each other; they seem to have trouble sharing cognitive thoughts. They speak quietly and use short, unenthusiastic terms, as they seem to be speaking a vocal form of shorthand. I realize that there are many engaging, well-spoken young people around, but their numbers are dwindling. The more impersonal the world becomes, the less our personalities flourish. Kids today are bombarded with electronic stimulation at every turn, which seems to trump in excitement that of a boring orator. My son and his friends can play video games for hours while barely a word is spoken, other than an occasional "oh yeah!" when they reach a new level. Are they learning the same vocal skills that I once did when I built tree forts with my friends? If we grunted our way through those projects, somebody would have gotten a nail to the head.

Kids still socialize at school, thank God, but how long will that last? We have meetings online, receive customer service through automated voice messages, and earn college degrees from the comfort of home. Eventually, the majority of high school students will receive their GED online. Many kids would love this alternative, Captain Crunch and the computer screen, all day, every day. Where new technology takes us next is anyone's guess, but losing our ability to communicate to actual people is a high price to pay.

Children learn to speak from their parents, and it is an important task to teach these skills. If a child's parents do not possess good auditory skills, then they will most likely suffer a similar fate. When slang and vulgarity is used in early development, then that same language will most likely be used by their children. Some kids break the pattern, but many never do. This would explain why a high school graduate can often be heard talking in a manner that makes practically no sense at all. How sad is it when you hear an athlete or a Miss America contestant who was educated right here in America being unable to convey a simple thought. Chances are good that their parents weren't famous orators giving motivational lectures. Our ability to communicate starts at home and is most useful when talking to God.

Many kids today spend way too much time inside as it would appear that the real world is having a hard time competing with the electronic virtual world. A constant electronic stimulant to the brain can make ordinary life seem boring to these kids. Their motor skills and muscular system suffer too, but that's for another time. Talking in general is boring to some of these kids, and without proper communication skills, a young person has a problematic future ahead. *"Cops"* is a popular television show that illustrates my point. Most criminals captured have one thing in common: they talk like Elmer Fudd with a softball stuck in their throat. Amazingly, most of the people being arrested on this program were educated right here in America and are left with little excuse.

Teachers should make it the top priority to instruct children to speak fluently when parents fail. However, that form of instruction is considered politically incorrect and no longer allowed. Telling a Southern kid to say "before" rather than "fur" could upset his heritage. If young girls use out of context, empty phrases to end every thought and a black kid never learns to correctly say the word "ask" then how can we expect them to learn physics? When we couple the lack of verbal instruction with an obvious electronic disconnect from reality, we are raising a generation of droids, and eventually, this breakdown of communication will lead to chaos. It won't be long before we will be speaking different languages of the same name in the same geographical regions. If we are not allowed to correct the speech patterns of children, we will eventually be back on the road to Babel.

We already have a large portion of Americans and illegal aliens who struggle to speak our national language. This communication hindrance causes problems every day in hospitals and businesses throughout the country. The problem is greatly enhanced when people who are raised in America and speak our native tongue lose a handle on the language. For the most part, you can still understand the person who uses heavy slang or the person whose speech pattern is limited to a certain geographical area, but for how long?

Part 2: Let Your Fingers Do the Talking

Laura Ingraham did a segment for Fox News one night where she went into a coffee shop to investigate the latest sensation of wireless computer chat. Amazingly, there were people chatting with others who were in the same two rooms—the physical room and the cyberspace room. Not reading the expressions or emotions on the faces of those we are communicating with will reduce our understanding of what a particular person is trying to convey. Eventually, we will become unable to understand true emotion altogether. I can't speak for everyone, but I've seen those science fiction movies about the future, and if we are headed into a world where our robots become our best friends, then you can go ahead and freeze me alongside Walt Disney until we come full circle.

A keyboard should be used as a tool, not our only link to the outside world. If a person texts his friend to invite him to dinner, it would make sense to have meaningful dialogue when they arrive or at least the ability to engage if the moment presents itself. I have seen couples having dinner in restaurants where one or the other spends the majority of the time either texting or chatting on their phone. Amazingly, when the phone is finally set aside, they usually remain silent, with the exception of a quiet word or two. If you text a particular friend for weeks on end while never actually speaking with that person, then the changes in voice pattern that might point to a real problem will be missed. Communicating is much more than words, and as a culture, we are rapidly losing our ability to understand each other, and this newfound destruction of communication is taking new forms.

Part 3: History Mystery

Pastor Rick Booye of Trail Christian Church in Eagle Point, Oregon once stated in a teaching of ultimate truth that, "Whoever wins the war writes the books, and that is true, but that doesn't mean that everybody who has won a war lies about it." Everyone has an agenda. My agenda in writing this book is to have the reader take God more seriously. If you don't like my agenda, then you can use this book to prop open a door or kill a fly. I'd prefer you give it to somebody who might care, but hey, it's your book.

Most College professors and other secular progressive thinkers have an agenda as well. They write and teach revisionary history all the time. They pick and choose what should and should not be taught, and in many cases delete altogether what they deem as unworthy to discuss. Who are they to decide what has value and what does not? Not only do they distort the truth, but they even attack language itself to assert their view. This is extremely dangerous territory in which we are currently setting up camp. If history and language cannot be trusted to some degree, then what are we left with? Simply stated; people who have obtained a position of power, who might feel that they have the better ideology, and who will look to erase opposing views for the common good. Ever heard of Ward Churchill? Examples of these criminal misdeeds are widespread, but I'm not a bean counter, remember? Luckily, these people are very easy to locate, and what they are illustrating as true might astound you.

Personally, I'm much more interested in why they distort the truth, rather than how. I could probably convince you that I was a former spy, because lying is in our nature and obviously the easy part, but hiding the agenda behind the lie is the tricky and more deceptive part. A blunt conclusion would imply that if people are looking for an escape clause to avoid God, guilt, and everything that comes with it, then why not have some company while fleeing. The more people who live in a world where morality takes a back seat and truth is purely relative to each individual, the less guilt will be felt by those who construct the lies in the first place.

Today, in the secular world, it is considered okay to sleep with another out of wedlock, but we didn't always think it was okay. Did we wake up one morning and suddenly change our opinion on what is right and wrong? Of course we didn't. It is a slow decline that comes from others telling you what is considered permissible. When we seek our answers from people who neglect God, we begin to lose whatever God has revealed to us for his purpose. How certain elitists can make a living determining the origin of morality is the question at hand. That will be discussed in a later chapter, but for now, we must realize that there are those who do not have your best interest at heart. They will use all their powers and multi-syllable words to confuse you at every turn and all of this will be done in the name of being smarter and more enlightened than you. You can leapfrog these peddlers of distorted knowledge simply by obtaining the fear of God. Who is wiser, a person who secures his eternal path or one who ignores it for power and pride and pushes his ideology on others, while denying opposing views?

Part 4: The Yes and No Debate

Nowhere is the artful skill of evading truth in conversation more prevalent than in the voice of an American politician. I can't speak for everyone, but it would be nice to hear a straight answer once in a while that isn't structured toward the latest polling data. Almost every American politician claims a belief in God, and in most cases it is the Christian God. It would be interesting to find out what they truly believe prior to their election, while leaving their evading skills at home for what I would consider a dream political debate. This could be done by the removal of microphones and placing the candidates in clear plastic cubicles where they could be seen, not heard. In front of each candidate would be three buttons: a red one for answering "no," a green one for answering "yes," and a gray one for refusing to answer. Each candidate would be allowed to push the gray button one time, but further refusal would eliminate them from running. I know that my rules are strict, but can't a guy have a dream?

So with the rules in place, the inquisition can begin, and hopefully somebody will grant me the first question. Assuming that we still have a country in 2016, I would venture to say that Mrs. Hillary Clinton will again be in the running, so I will direct my interrogation at her.

Question #1

Secretary Clinton, do you believe that the Bible is the inspired word of God?

She would feel safe to press the green button and answer "yes," because she has proclaimed this belief before.

Question #2

Secretary Clinton, since you believe that the Bible is the inspired word of God and it says that homosexuality is an abomination; do you agree with Jesus that it is?

Here she would probably reach for the grey button and hope for an easier question.

Question #3

Secretary Clinton, do you believe Jesus is pro choice?

This is where Mrs. Clinton would leave the debate and we could rid ourselves, once and for all, of her backwards stance.

This mock debate was not to pick on "old Hillary." Okay, maybe it was to a point, but the same scenario could be acted out with virtually every politician in Washington. Politicians hate yes-and-no questions and will blather on and on in lieu of the answer until we forget what the question was in the first place. If we instituted a debate system like the one above, eventually we would be electing persons who would have little if anything to hide. They wouldn't be hindered by lobbyists and activists, because their belief system will have been transparent from the get-go. The most talented communicators among us are usually politicians, and yet we have zero idea what they truly believe, simply because they fear losing their next election. That is a sad part of American culture.

Just a Thought #6

Lack of communication is one of our greatest fears. It is used as a form of punishment in prisons, as the inmates dreadfully fear spending time in "the hole" or solitary confinement. When I was a kid, I used to watch the claymation television show *Davey and Goliath*. One particular episode found Davey stuck in a boxcar alone, heading out of town on the tracks. After he was finally rescued, Goliath asked him, "Gee, Davey, weren't you scared being all alone?" to which Davey replied, "I wasn't really alone, Goliath. God was with me." You can avoid solitude your entire life, but in the end there is one dance you'll do alone. Knowledge of God's love is a good thing to have at that point.

Part 5: Trusted Words

No one has the right to choose what is wrong.

Abraham Lincoln

We all rely on the authority of others to obtain certain ideas in which we have come to believe as true. I've never been to Hawaii, but I take it on authority of others that it exists. We all need to trust some things that we cannot know with absolute certainty to be true. We all do it, all the time, and when you really break it down, most of what we believe stems from others. We, as individuals, merely decide whether they are a reliable source or not. If a door-to-door salesman tells you that his magical solution will remove rust with a quick wipe of a rag, you probably won't believe it without a demonstration. If your father tells you the same thing, it may be much more believable, unless your father *is* a door-to-door salesman and borrows money from you every other day and never pays you back. In that unfortunate case, I'd insist on the demonstration.

We as humans have the ability to discern through logic and reason to find our conclusions, but we use the authority of others in our inquisition much more than we realize. Tragically, 40 million babies have been aborted since Roe v Wade, and Planned Parenthood has performed many of these abortions. Through logic, reason, and limited research, I have concluded that they are a distasteful organization, and I'm being nice. My logic and reason are limited because I have no empirical knowledge of these findings. I was not present to count the abortions, and I haven't conducted any studies of Planned Parenthood workers and the advice given to their clients. I purely rely on the authority of others whom I trust to tell me what is true. I could be wrong, but it would take contrary evidence from other people whom I trust to convince me otherwise. I haven't found any reliable evidence contrary to my conclusion, so for now the organization will remain destructive in my mind.

So how do we decide what to believe and what to regard as fallacy? First we can use our own tools of deduction to search the agenda of others. Secondly, we can assume that our gut and our hearts are, for the most part, reliable. Finally, we can use the laws of nature to determine if what is being laid out in front of us makes natural sense.

A quick look into history would lead us to believe that naturally the Disciples would have remained hidden to save their own skins, but remarkably and in stark contrast to what would make natural sense; they defied human nature and offered themselves to the slaughter for what they believed in. Something amazing happened at that point in human history that changed their nature. I can conclude that at the very least, they believed Jesus was God. Logic and reason would lead me to believe that they knew Jesus was God. These tools of reason and deduction are limited and will only get us to a certain point. Therefore, when deciding ultimate truth, we must seek out a higher authority. We are welcome to use our God-given tools in our search, but we are limited in knowledge and require faith. Many answers are revealed to us from the Creator, but in the end, we will be required to trust that God is the ultimate decider and that his judgment is perfect.

Part 6: The Road to Cleveland

Before we move away from the decay in our communication, I thought that I might amuse you with a story that happened not long ago. In the shadowy world of customer service, Americans are usually left hanging on the wrong end of the telephone line, hyperventilating, gritting our teeth, and basically wishing for a mystical way to climb through the telephone line to the person on the other end and fully display our frustrations. This frustration is even further enhanced when dealing with government officials who are protected by tenure and who seem to have little concern about time and the people using theirs in hope of a solution. If you actually take the time to meet and greet government employees and are looking for answers to your questions, then your frustration will lead to madness, and possibly physical illness.

This story takes place in a not-so-distant summer, when I had heard of a construction prospect in Cleveland, Ohio. A particular mortgage broker (who shall remain unnamed) had informed a friend of mine and me that there was a shortage of HUD housing in the city of Cleveland, and that if we were willing to remodel some dilapidated buildings, we would find that there were some amazing profits to be made. The formula was simple: we would find the building, the broker would secure the financing, we would do the work, and all three parties would share in the profits once the building was filled with government-backed tenants. In order to complete this process, somebody needed to find one such building to get the ball rolling. Unfortunately for me, I found myself headed to Cleveland in the heat of July with a truck full of tools. It had been my intention to purchase a storage container for the tools and avoid any further travel that was not by air. Steve, the young apprentice that I mentioned earlier, decided to join in the venture east, hoping to end the lull in construction that we were experiencing at the time.

Upon arriving in Cleveland, we met with a Realtor, who showed us several buildings, most of which were rendered beyond repair in my mind. When you find yourself looking at the interior of a hundred-year-old brick building and you cannot decipher which room was formerly the kitchen, it's probably time to say "Next!" Some of these buildings were actually missing their stairwells, but all of them were missing their cabinets, plumbing, wiring, heaters, and fixtures. Basically, they were gutted, and the only remnants were broken bottles of beer and the bloodstains from the fisticuffs that had once ensued. There was human waste on every floor, and rats that could hold their own against any army of neighborhood cats. To say the very least, Steve and I were tremendously depressed, and our hope of finding the right building was quickly waning. Then we had a stroke of luck; the final building that we were scheduled to see was in every way the opposite of our previous horrors. This building actually had working toilets, and the wiring had not been ripped from the walls. Most of the windows remained unbroken, and while old and in need of repair, the cabinets were in place. The only major repair needed to transform this building into a viable home for tenants was a twenty-by-ten-foot section of the front eave that had collapsed downward upon itself. This was an easy fix, and I estimated the cost for renovating the entire building at around fifty thousand dollars. With the asking price of twenty-eight thousand, it seemed like we had a winner.

The building had eight large units, and the HUD housing department would secure between nine hundred and twelve hundred dollars monthly for each unit. After the building was approved for housing, it could be sold for an estimated four hundred thousand or could simply be used for income of the secure nature.

Before I reveal how this apparently sweet deal fell apart, I need to tell you the amusing part of the story and the part that is relevant to the breakdown of communication. Steve and I had found our building, but we needed to know exactly what was required by the HUD organization in order to make our building ready for occupancy. We used the GPS to find a county phone number, and they directed us to our first location on the east side of Cleveland. When we arrived, we found a large group of individuals waiting in line for their weekly checks, and not to say that we stood out in that crowd, but it might have been as easy to spot us standing in that line as it would be to find Kareem Abdul-Jabbar on a playground basketball court teaching seven-year-olds how to do layups. When it was finally our turn to be helped, the lady behind the counter had zero idea what we were talking about and simply circled an address on a pamphlet and said that we needed to ask for Shirley.

When we arrived at the next location, just outside of downtown, we found a building that appeared vacant, and to be completely truthful, kind of scary. We approached with caution and slowly opened the doors to this single-story dry-rotted building. Inside, we found four people sitting behind desks, chatting with each other and doing their best to ignore us. Eventually, one lady who remained comfortably seated placed her hand over the phone and literally shouted at us, "What do you guys want?" We explained that we were looking for Shirley and that hopefully she could answer some of our questions about HUD housing requirements. She quickly replied that there was no Shirley that she had ever heard of, but if we wanted answers about the HUD requirements, we needed to talk to Tim Jenkins (I truthfully cannot remember his name, so this will have to do) who was in charge of every aspect of the program. She then grabbed another pamphlet that matched the one I already had and circled a different address, flung it at me, and then turned away without saying a word. I remember Steve saying, "What a witch," as our frustration was quickly turning into a demented form of humor.

When we arrived at our final location, a towering skyscraper in downtown, we really believed that this guy Tim would answer all our questions and put an end to our aimless wandering. Tim's office was on the fifteenth floor, and when we opened the door, we found a cozy waiting room with comfortable chairs in which we were instructed to sit and wait for Tim to join us. After about ten minutes, Tim opened the door and walked into the room. Tim was an African-American guy in his middle fifties, with short hair and a graying beard. He was a small guy, a little heavy, and had apparently just finished lunch, because prior to reaching out to shake my hand, he covered his mouth and had his first of many silent belches. The remaining part of this conversation can be best displayed in a dialogue between the two of us, as I can remember it almost verbatim.

Tim: "What can I do for ya?"

Robert: "I was hoping that you could help me with the construction requirements for renovating possible HUD housing."

Tim (After a look of confusion and another silent belch): "We just get the list of people in need of housing, and that's all we do."

Robert: "Uhhh, I was told that you were in charge of the HUD program here in Cleveland."

Tim: "Well, that's true, but ya see, we just get the list and that's all we do."

Okay, so at this point, Steve is about to burst into laughter. His face is red, his eyes are watering, and he is sucking in all the air his lungs can contain to keep his composure. A quick glance at Steve and his 100 percent focus on not laughing instantly put me in the same condition, but I needed to focus on my questions.

Robert: "Well, Tim, where would I go to find some of the answers I need?"

Tim (Silent belch): "I'm really not sure, 'cause like I said, we just get the list ..."

Robert (This time I finished the equation for him.): "And that's all you do."

That was it for Steve; he had transformed into werewolf or something. Veins were popping out on his forehead, his face seemed to be swelling, and his entire body was shivering, as he appeared to be trying to hold back the waters of Niagara Falls. I've seen people trying to hold back laughter before, but Steve was taking this task to a newfound level. A moment before we both lost it, Tim performed his final silent belch, slapped his hands loudly upon his knees, slowly rose from his chair, reached out his hand to shake mine, and said, and I quote, "I hep I heped ya," and left the room. Tim apparently had found it convenient somewhere in his past to morph the words *help* and *hope* into one, and this was the final straw that had Steve and me rolling down the hallway as we left the office.

When we eventually calmed down, we had come to the realization that we had spent an entire afternoon attempting to find our answers and were left with the astonishing fact that the head of the department of HUD housing in the city of Cleveland gets a list. The breakdown of communication here was amazing. Obviously, somebody knew more than Tim but failed to communicate these facts to him. Also, it can be deduced that there was a failure in communication between the first lady we spoke with and Shirley, who was never told that she doesn't really exist. Finally, we should concede that second lady we spoke with had sent many persons to Tim's office, and with her ill-tempered demeanor, they were never to return.

The mortgage broker who started this whole debacle did an about face when I returned home with a solid prospect in hand. She had presided over several meetings with me and a few other interested parties prior to my venture in which she filled her office with optimistic blather. She would look out at all present and say that the lenders she had in mind will "simply love you guys." She said that we were such wonderful and caring people and so obviously capable that lending will not be an issue. This particular broker, who had mystical Eastern philosophical sayings on every wall in her office, had nothing but praise and adoration for everybody who aspired to partake in this partnership. Apparently, she didn't expect to be taken seriously, because when I had completed the first step in finding the building, her attitude changed dramatically. My friend and proposed partner informed me the day of my return that the broker didn't want to deal with me because she found me rude and untrustworthy. I thought he was kidding, and he had to assure me several times that he wasn't, before I believed him. He said that it was something that I had said at one of the meetings that set her off, but she couldn't remember what. Neither could anyone else, for that matter.

Excluding the broker, there were five persons present at each of those meetings, and not a single one could remember me saying anything unpleasant in any way. We did, however, remember her adoration for me and the compliments she showered me with, but we were left without explanation for her about face. It has been my experience that people entrenched in mystical thought are egomaniacs, disguised with loving words based in humility. She most assuredly could not obtain the financing required and needed to place the blame elsewhere. Since she had an existing professional relationship with my friend, I was the easy target. She is two things: an egotistical mystical muse and an unequivocal liar in which I have no use.

In conclusion: We are blessed with the ability to communicate. Without this blessing, we would merely rely on instincts, and they can often be wrong. We wouldn't know or care what another person might be feeling, and our existence would be reduced to the food chain. Humans wouldn't be long for this dangerous world without our superior brains. Fortunately, we do have superior brains, and it doesn't require vast deductions to realize that we are special and set apart. We are meant to communicate with one another and with God. At first, God spoke to man directly. When we learned to read and write, he dropped us note, and eventually he paid us a visit. God has always been trying to reach us, and he is persistent. Unfortunately, we have abused our ability to communicate, through lies and distortion, and we have disconnected human emotion and the personal spoken word in our new technological age. The saddest part of the communication breakdown is that many have forgotten to talk to God. He gave us the purely human ability to speak and listen, and he deserves our attention.

Chapter 9

Planning to Go Somewhere

Part 1: Our Plan vs. God's Plan

Aim at heaven and you will get earth thrown in. Aim at earth and you will get neither.

C. S. Lewis

When we put our trust in God and his sovereignty, it eliminates our worries of ultimate destiny. It's the meantime that so many struggle with. I would suggest *The Purpose-Driven Life* by Rick Warren to any Christian struggling with what direction to take. I have a few thoughts, however, for those who haven't put their trust in a higher power. God made the board game we call "planet Earth," and he controls the pieces. Wherever you currently are, that is where you are meant to be at this particular moment. God has a plan, and we will play our part, whether we like it or not. What about free will? That is a question best left to the experts, but I can tell you this: we do have free will, but God already knows what we will choose. Every choice we make will fit perfectly into his plan until his will is done. I will admit that this is an amazing concept, but I believe it to be true.

The problem that most people have with this concept is in our limited dimension of time. God is not subject to our dimensions of space and time. In fact, he dwells in ways that are well beyond our understanding. Believe it or not, God did not wait forever to create the world; it just seems that way to us because it appears that he created the universe at a particular time. Time is part of creation, and therefore doesn't need to exist outside of our perceived physical realm. If you take God as truth, then he had no beginning and time didn't come into existence until we did. The Creation had a beginning, and time was part of it, but God is separate from time and the Creation. Simply put, one cannot create oneself. Basically, we need to temporarily remove God from his work to understand this idea. Many theologians might argue this point, but I believe that God doesn't see each event unfold one after the other. I think that God sees the world as it is, period!

C. S. Lewis put our perception of time eloquently in *Mere Christianity.*

Lewis illustrates his idea that God does not dwell in the created time and that every moment for God is the present. This of course answers the age old question of God being able to answer untold numbers of prayers at the same time that they are being offered to him.

Lewis then offers an analogy that further illustrates the point. He uses a writer's perspective of being the creator of his characters within his work of literature. In being the creator he is not bound to the time that exists within the pages and therefore can be at liberty to rest between sentences while the characters have no knowledge of the resting periods because of their created time restraints.

Just because God knows our inevitable choice, we shouldn't be caught up in the notion that our actions don't matter. They do. Remember, we are part of Creation and we are therefore limited to the created dimensions. If I knew that I was going to choose your construction company to replace my kitchen cabinets, it shouldn't affect your price or professionalism, unless I told you beforehand. God knows the outcome, but we don't. When we are teetering on the threshold of accepting God, he will beckon us and encourage us to make the right decision and he can do this using time as we know it and at the same instant be dwelling out of time altogether. There are many books on physics pertaining to dimensions, and *time* permitting; you might want to read one. A deep understanding of physics is not critical to faith, but a basic understanding can help answer some of the more troubling skeptical questions. I have slowly obtained the general idea, but I'm far from an expert. I can tell you this, however: every action you take, whether good or bad, is in accordance with God's plan.

A troubling issue will come to the forefront when we try to instill our plan over God's. It is impossible to do, and whatever actions we take will work perfectly for God's purpose, even if we fight him tooth and nail through the process. If we destroy ourselves or oppress the meek, it will still be working toward God's end. Not everyone will find everlasting life, for it is written that the path to the kingdom is a narrow one, and the other well beaten. God wants that "no man should perish," but in giving us choice, he knew it would have consequences. Love, by definition, requires choice; therefore, our love would be tainted if we were forced to love rather than to give love freely. He gives his love freely and he gives us the freedom to love him back. Trying to make sense of how God works will probably give you a headache, and it will remain a mystery for the most part anyway, but knowing that God gives you what you need to know in order to have a relationship with him should be enough to satisfy you. Besides, he never promised you the blueprints to the universe, and you wouldn't understand them anyway.

Part 2: Sunday Morning Sidewalk

On a typical Sunday morning, Americans are a busy bunch. Some are headed to a church service, while others are seeking pleasure elsewhere. People hike, swim, watch movies, have barbecues, and simply relax. It is still considered the day of rest, inasmuch as many people are not working. Everybody's going somewhere with a hope that they find satisfaction to whatever suits their fancy, and the choices seem endless. Worshipping God, reading his Word, and the fellowship that follows can be a beautiful thing to a believer. For a secularist or for the non-committed person, walking around a lakeside trail might be pleasing. For others, doing drugs and stealing cars might be in their day's plan. Maybe cheating on one's spouse while they are at church might make the pocket planner. Unfortunately, the last two choices detailed here are normally chosen by the secularist or the non-committed.

A person who has truly committed his life to a higher power will usually try his best to please that higher power. If God gave you the ability to determine right from wrong, then you have little excuse when laying out the day's plan. I really don't think that a large portion of society is giving their actions the respect they deserve. I don't think that a single mother of three who invites her boyfriend of two months to move in and play house is really thinking about her decision. She is focused on her wants and is being helped and deceived by bad forces. When her daughter is molested by the boyfriend and he then steals her car and never returns, she plays dumb. She looks in every direction for compassion, and as a Christian I would give her compassion, but not without instruction. A single devout Christian mother of three would know what God desires. She probably wouldn't introduce her children to her boyfriend until shortly before the wedding, and she would be sure that he was a godly man who would help teach her children right from wrong in a safe and caring way.

Every time we fall further apart from God with our choices, it becomes harder to find God. Think about it this way: if every time you made a bad choice, you lost a piece of your heart, eventually it would stop beating and you would die. That is essentially what happens. It is true that God can save the most wretched of people, like the slave master in *Amazing Grace* or even a Christian persecutor like Paul of Taurus but it won't happen for all of us. Basically, what you choose matters. Even if you do not currently know God, doing the right thing—which is indicated by your emotional response to your actions—will put you in a better place to find God. I've known the sweetest people who were clueless as to the knowledge of God, while on the other hand, I've known people choking in pride and perversion who thought they truly knew God and were in step with his will. God is caring and patient, and when seeking him, he is easier to find when we emulate his nature. It would be my guess that the sweet people would find the shorter path, because they seem to have more humility and their decisions are not as rigid. Whatever you choose to do this Sunday, remember this: You can make the plan and choose the course, but you cannot find any lasting fulfillment without intervention from above.

Part 3: How Great Art Thou?

Are you destined for greatness? Who determines greatness? I believe that Darin Erstad is a great ballplayer because he plays the game right and with integrity. If he didn't have any talent, then my statement wouldn't make any sense. Stating the obvious is not required if it is assumed that the person I'm talking with knows who Darin Erstad is, and if the person I am talking with has similar values, they will most likely agree. Barry Bonds had unbelievable talent, but I can't call him a great ballplayer because he cheated (allegedly) and he played with a lack of integrity as noted by his numerous teammates. Another person who may not share my similar values might argue the point. Greatness is in the eye of the beholder; therefore, if you feel that you are bound for greatness or that greatness has already labeled you the king of something considered worthy, keep the following in focus. When you compare your greatness in contrast to a God who gave you two opposing thumbs, then exactly how great are you?

People like to judge each other on the playing fields of life. "I scored the most points" or "I donated more money." Whatever the case might be, we weigh ourselves against the abilities and attributes of other people all the time. If we see ourselves as a leader of the pack, we assure ourselves that we must be making the right decisions. Eventually, our egos will inflate and we will soon believe that it was our ability to choose correctly that put us in our advantageous position. God, on the other hand, doesn't keep score. He looks at sin as bad, period. He wishes to deflate our ego and make us more useful in his plan. It is for this particular reason that I believe a person has a better chance of finding

God with a humble and caring attitude rather than a mean-spirited one. Making it easier is not to say that it is your attitude that puts you in the right boat. You will be either a willing participant in his kingdom or not.

Part 4: Seekers

I had a particular friend who would act like Superman swimming in liquefied kryptonite whenever God was mentioned in conversation. He would actually cover his ears like a child while chanting, "I don't want to hear it," over and over again. We played on the same softball team, and although we saw each other every Friday for years, other than over softball and pizza, I really didn't know him well. I had seen his aversion to the God topic on a few separate occasions, but he never let on why. Many people hate talking about God for reasons I have already discussed, but this guy had a past, and it probably wasn't a pretty one. I finally had the chance to ask him about it between games of a daylong tournament. I really didn't get too much out of him, just the basics. He had lost a parent early in life, and he saw another battle many addictions. He had a perception of what he considered good people having tremendous turmoil in their lives, and he had his own as well. He said he used to believe in God, but not anymore. I told him that believing in something and putting faith in something are two separate things, and then I asked him if he truly knew God and if he ever read his words. He hadn't. I knew the answer before I asked, because I find it hard to swallow that a person who stakes their claim in eternal ideas rather than the temporal ones could lose their faith. In fact, my faith tells me that it is impossible to do.

In other words, the doors to heaven only swing one way. Basically, he was a seeker who stopped seeking. I lost track of him a few years back, but hopefully he has renewed his search. Oddly, he is further along than many other seekers. At least he was on the right track, in that he once believed there is a God. If a person is on the wrong track, then as C. S. Lewis says, not only do they need to find the right track to obtain what they desire, they must first back off the wrong tracks. Some people make the journey much longer than it needs to be. I will still tend to give all seekers, regardless of which track they're on, much more credit than the apathetic person who steers clear of the tracks altogether. People who show little or no concern about their eternal future are beyond my understanding.

Imagine yourself in Virginia City in the middle of the nineteenth century. You own a large piece of land and you intend to mine it for silver. You hire workers to dig the mine, and they've made vast tunnels throughout your land. Unfortunately, they have yet to strike silver. Many will become discouraged, and their work will suffer. You, on the other hand, have faith that the mine will eventually pay off, and you continue the search. One by one, the workers leave, knowing that the greater portions of their pay will arrive when the silver is found. Eventually, it is down to you and your sons to continue the search alone. Day after day, week after week, you dig. It is tiresome work, and eventually you run out of money, but your faith in finding the treasure doesn't wane; you simply find work elsewhere and continue your search whenever time allows. Twenty years later, your wife has left you for a businessman in San Francisco and your boys have grown and left as well. Still, you have faith and continue your search. Eventually, after years of toiling, you strike it big. You find a silver vein that appears to reach for miles. Your search, through years of toiling, was not in vain.

God is very much like the mine. He has untold riches for those who persistently search to find him. His mine has already been purchased for us, and he will reward the faithful. So many will fall by the wayside like the workers and the family, but of those who remain faithful he will be well pleased. The true treasure is eternal life in God's kingdom. Silver and other worldly riches could never compare to what we are, in essence, truly searching for. God promises you that if you seek him, you will find him, as well as your place in his kingdom. If your only desire is the silver and its purchasing power, then you will be disappointed in the end, but for those who seek heaven, they will never be let down.

If it is true that God emptied himself into human form, walked among us, died and rose again, shouldn't all who hear this mind-blowing story be curious as to what he had to say? Even if you feel that the whole biblical theme is absurd, the pure fact that millions around the world believe the scriptures to be the inspired Word of God should strike your curiosity. Not having an answer to your own existence, as many do not, should expand on that curiosity.

Now imagine that you work for Microsoft. You and fifty others work in a tucked-away segment of a large building, miles away from the corporate headquarters. Your office deals with petty details and the VIPs of the company rarely make an appearance. Bill Gates himself hasn't made a personal appearance at your office in the fifteen years that you have been employed. You have spent the first half of your working life at a corporation and you have never met the guy in charge. You've heard a lot about him and seen him from your nosebleed seats at company events, but you don't know him personally and you don't really care. You realize that he has your working future in his hands, but you feel that it is beyond your concern, simply because there's nothing you can do about it anyway.

Then one evening you get food poisoning. It must have been the chicken; it's always the chicken. Anyway, after a night in the bathroom, you call in sick the next day and play video games and take two naps. As your pure bad luck would have it, this just happened to be the same day and the first day that Mr. Gates decided to spend six hours meeting and greeting your office colleagues while discussing the future of your department. The following day, your colleagues are renewed with a gleeful purpose in what they are doing. Everybody seems foreign to you. Jim isn't complaining about the lack of staples, Sherry isn't complaining about not being noticed, and your immediate boss isn't complaining about Jim and Sherry and their petty problems, and amazingly, he isn't yelling at anybody else. Something's afoot. Your associates will be quick to indulge you in the details of what you had missed and speak with delight of the bright future ahead. They feel a need to, and most likely you will be eager to hear about it. If, on the other hand, you don't care about what you missed and actually avoid any discussion of your personal future within the company, then you are acting like an apathetic, spoiled child, but not unlike the multitudes of people who throughout the last two millennia have avoided the gospels.

You have the ability to know what you missed, and you were born with curiosity, but you can't seem to find yourself caring. Whatever was learned the day before affects you directly, but it appears easier to you to ignore it and go on as before and leave the blissful feel-good attitude to others who do care. If you were to know about the preceding day's events and the promise that was detailed, then you might be forced to change something about your daily duties, and you're not quite ready.

This same scenario has been played out like a broken record for two thousand years. God walked among us and gave us some really good news. Some got the information firsthand, while others believed it on the authority of others—coupled with the revealed truth in written history. Today, many are unwilling to hear the good news while they seem to be too involved with the here and now to concern themselves with the hereafter. People who know the good news are being persistent in conveying the news to the apathetic masses, and ironically, that makes them the annoying ones. Unfortunately for those who avoid the truth, people who have obtained the truth are not easily discouraged. They will continue to spread the message until their dying breath. I should know because I'm one of them. God will give you his gift of grace until your dying breath, but the clock is ticking and your destiny is in the balance.

Part 5: Trusting the Road Ahead

As I understand the Christian religion, it was, and is, a revelation.

John Adams

People have legitimate questions that can only be answered with trust. I have a brother-in-law who is currently serving in Afghanistan, and he submitted to me a list of questions from several soldiers who were serving in his battalion. The questions came from a group of non-believers and they were pre-written and scripted. It was obvious that many Christian groups had reached out to them, and having the toughest questions armed and ready for e-mail made it easy to respond and to get these joy-filled people off their backs. I love these types of questions; they are challenging and will provoke much-needed discussion. Unfortunately, some questions can only be answered with the word *trust*. If a person doesn't have the trust of God, then the answers will fall on deaf ears. The question that remains etched in my mind is the one that requires trust over substance to the greatest degree.

From an American soldier:

If I believe that I'm going to heaven because I believe in Jesus, then what about an enemy combatant that I kill who believes in the Muslim God and who has never been taught that Jesus is the one and only God? Will they be sentenced to hell just because they were born in a different geographical region? If they are true to their faith and it is all they have ever known, should they be punished for it?

To answer this question without insisting that the inquisitor have a complete trust in God is not going to score well. I have a guess as to how God will judge, but I have complete trust that he will be perfectly just. I would guess that God would judge the Muslim soldier who has never heard of Jesus differently than an American soldier who has been infiltrated with the word from all corners of the globe. If your family and friends have been trying to inform you about their faith, which is endearing to them, and that you can have it too, then your excuses will be limited. If you continue to run away from hearing the message, then I believe that God may be less forgiving when your time comes. I believe that God is in control and that he is all-knowing and perfectly just. Therefore, I trust that he will judge according to his will. As a believer, it is all about spreading the Word, and it is promised that the Word will be heard by all. If believers do not reach certain individuals, then we must trust that God will.

In conclusion, we all have a choice to make. Living in the free world, our blessed life affords us many luxuries but little excuse. God would be the kind of boss who might say "My way or the highway," and doesn't leave anything open to discussion. We have limited free will, and everything we do, good or bad, is going to work for the good of

God's plan. If we tend to *our will* while avoiding God's, then we will be held in self-bondage, and in many cases not even know it. If we come to realize that *our will* is flawed and we admit this to God, then and only then can we experience the true freedom of emulating, though not perfectly, God's will.

Just a Thought #7

Fear of the unknown is understandable. Everyone is nervous their first day on a new job. These fears can be subdued by a general knowledge of what is to come. Death is among our most common fears, but having knowledge of God and faith in his plan will erase that fear. By no means does it free you from a fear of how you will die or what will be left undone, but you will rest easy knowing your inevitable destiny.

Chapter 10

God, the Great Scientist

Science without religion is lame. Religion without science is blind.

Albert Einstein

Part 1: Designed Intelligence

We hear it all the time: God has no place in the classroom. If 85 percent of people believe in some form of God, then it would make sense to believe that he created all the matter that makes up a classroom. It's his room; who are we to expel him? Sam Walton is dead, but if he were alive today I doubt that many would say that he has no place in a local Wal-Mart. There are thousands upon thousands of books that will go into great detail explaining why intelligent design is the only plausible explanation for our existence. The mere fact that you have two opposing thumbs to hold one of those books should be evidence enough to put the matter to rest. Years of lies and multi-syllable words bouncing around our brains like a marble in the dryer have led us to be more skeptical then our forefathers.

Skeptical books that lead to a naturalistic point of view offer no plausible answers, but they do offer plenty of excuses. Hitler and Stalin

91

were naturalists, and they used their world view to excuse their mass slaughter of millions. They were simply weeding out the less fit, and they had no one to answer to and believed that science gave them an excuse for their atrocities. It does require some faith to have a relationship with God, but it requires a giant leap of faith to believe in the naturalistic world view. A person requires humility to believe in a Creator but to share the opposing view; humility is only for the person above you on the ladder. After you reach the top, as was the case with Hitler and Stalin, then humility is lost altogether. This is a dangerous precedent, and history proves the point time and time again. If a person is put in charge of others and doesn't have the fear of answering to a higher power, then pride can transform them into a monster.

I've always marveled at the secular world's ability to dismiss science when it directly points to design. On the other hand, they will cling to age-old theories and fight tooth and nail to pass this information down to future generations. Opposing views to naturalism are demonized at every level of academia and are rapidly becoming extinct in all other areas of the culture as well. If college professors really wanted to get to the bottom of things, they would welcome all ideas into the discussion. Obviously, they don't, and therefore we are left to accept that they don't want to know the opposing view or they fear ending their passionate love affair with their loophole. Secularists love excuses, while God-fearing people realize they don't have one.

God is the original scientist, and he gave us brains to unravel many mysteries. Still, some mysteries will never be solved. Evolution is a simple theory that tries to explain our existence naturally, but the theory has more potholes then an unpaved road in the poor part of Tijuana. Unfortunately, many college graduates never see the holes and simply fall right in. Read the other side of the issue and you will quickly see the absurdities that evolution contains. If you are one of many who think that we evolved from nothing and that naturalistic forces started the ball in motion, then you need to ask yourself a question: Did the theory of evolution answer all your questions about life or did it just make your personal shortcomings a little easier to swallow? If evolution didn't leave you with more questions, then you are either a non inquisitive person or a liar, which of course, is no big deal to a naturalist.

Part 2: When Science Points to Design

People use science all the time to deny any form of a deity. If science points toward a designer during a debate on origins, secularists will simply turn to name-calling or throw a pie at you. We learn at an early age that, try as you might, you can't have it both ways.

Laura Ingraham, Bill O'Reilly, Sean Hannity, Rush Limbaugh, David Limbaugh, Ann Coulter and many others have several things in common. For one, they all make their living seeking the truth and informing others of their findings. Secondly, they are all human and have many flaws in their characters. Finally, they all have a belief in the God of the Bible and are quick to admit their personal flaws. Others, who make a living distorting the truth share many commonalties as well. (You know who they are, and I don't want to be sued) First off, they have a hard time excepting their personal flaws. Secondly, they lie about others with opposing views and finally, they mock Christianity at every chance presented to them.

I am intrigued to say the least when I find that so many people in my personal life respect the political and social opinions of Christian personalities in the limelight, but never wish to inquire about their religious beliefs. If a person who makes a living seeking truth usually becomes a Christian at some point during their lives, where as those who distort truth usually never do, maybe we should all take notice of this undeniable fact.

In regards to a belief in the God of the Bible and a denouncing of absurd naturalistic ideas, I find it most interesting that most of the fore mentioned individuals above are rarely challenged on their writing. Ann Coulter wrote some blistering and scathing details about the lies perpetrated by the proponents' of evolution over the years in her book "Godless". She then went on a book tour where she was in the company of many secularists who can barely tolerate her, little yet her views. A rational thinking person might conclude that this would be a perfect opportunity for a person with an opposing view point to offer an argument. Sadly, the argument never comes; it is left to float in suspended animation in lieu of an attack of how she presented her point in a mean-spirited way.

Ann Coulter presented to the entire world that most of the attributes to furthering the evolutionary cause were in fact lies and yet nobody challenged her. (At least to my knowledge) Why is that? If a person does not have an answer to well documented facts and those particular facts are working against their cause, what will remain as a defense? Attacking the way somebody tells the truth is their only game plan, but unfortunately that doesn't negate the truth to the rational and logical thinker: it merely clouds the minds of the individuals who are quick to dismiss the information out of hatred of the writer in the first place.

Ever wonder why there are forces that are trying to distort history, language, and the very meanings of words? When logic and reason do not fit neatly into their safe haven, they attempt to destroy logic and reason altogether. They do this because it is much easier than facing the truth head-on. It has become very apparent that when faced with hardcore facts, many choose to either ignore the facts or challenge their validity with invalid theories. Science has been their ally for years, but now scientists are turning away from the naturalistic world view. This awakening is happening at a rapid pace, and therefore it is leaving many people in a dismal gray area. If naturalism is removed from the secularist viewpoint, they will be left courting Alice in a fictitious place called Wonderland, and it is anyone's guess where they will go from there.

Most logical-thinking scientists agree that the universe had a beginning. If there was a beginning, then there had to be a beginner. Beginning=beginner, that's logical. If you believe that the universe had a beginning and not a beginner, then you might as well concede that logic doesn't exist at all. Most logical-thinking scientists also believe in the second law of thermodynamics: "All matter if left to its own accord will go from a state of present order to lesser order or entropy." I like to think of this law in a practical way. If an infant is abandoned, it will die because it will not receive the nurturing required to sustain life. Although with nourishment, the infant will develop, but it is still on a crash course with inevitable decay. All the nutrition in the world won't keep us alive forever; it will merely delay the process. The same can be said of an orange. It will ripen to a point, but will eventually fall off the branch and rot. At the point that an orange rots, all the king's horses and all the king's men will not be able to make desirable orange juice out of it.

In the end, we must realize that all life forms are in decay. Portions of life forms have the ability to heal, but they will leave a scar, whether you see it or not. Overall and certainly after development, all things go from greater order to less order. This law is contrary in every way to the naturalistic point of view. In order to evolve, we must first reverse this law and allow for a guy like Al Franken to eventually evolve into a person like Bill O'Reilly. Secularists simply ignore contrary findings or offer little or no explanation to this physical law. What is convenient to their viewpoint is to be taken as factual. What doesn't fit is not up for discussion.

We can learn much about our Creator through creation as the universe is an open textbook. An attempt was and is being made to close the textbooks by Charles Darwin enthusiasts, or as Ann Coulter calls them "Darwaniacs." Sadly, for many this case is already closed, the judge has long since retired, and the jury of their peers is helping them celebrate. Secularists have been slamming the classroom doors on theists for decades now, and they are intent on winning the battle. Whatever we learn about God will not be learned in school because if any theology is taught in school, it will be a pluralistic viewpoint that all beliefs are equally valid. Any opposing views on origins apart from the naturalistic view would be considered a concession and discussed with contempt. If the ancient Greeks pondered these questions of origin and destiny, maybe we should as well. If we are evolving or simply becoming more aware, as a logical person might see it, shouldn't we be welcoming new findings? Are we going to let a theory that holds little validity end all discussion? Darwin himself wouldn't believe his own theory if he had knowledge of our information. He said it himself in his writings. Look it up!

To know God, you must learn what he revealed about himself, but to believe that there is a God, you only need to look around you. Design is yelling at you from every mountaintop and in the faces of people you see every day. There are those who will continue to deny a Creator, but they cannot use logic and reason to promote their conclusions. They are mired in the past and are losing the argument. Whenever a person begins to lose an argument, he has two choices: concede or attack. The attack is in full force, and I don't see a concession anywhere on the horizon.

Matter cannot be created or destroyed by humans. We can scramble matter in a hurry with a nuclear bomb, but that doesn't mean the scrambled matter ceases to exist. Scientists mostly agree with this first law of thermodynamics as well. It then becomes interesting when we realize that if there is a Creator, at some point he must have stopped creating, based on the fact that there is no new matter. If we believe that life simply formed naturally, then it wouldn't make sense that life would naturally cease to exist. Life forms die and decay, and their once-beautiful existence is transformed to ashes and finally dust, but try as you might, you cannot make the dust disappear from the universe. Only a Creator can remove what was once created, therefore If you believe what Carl Sagan said at the beginning of his TV show, *Cosmos,* "The universe is all there is and all there ever will be." Then you are living a sad existence that will end badly.

In conclusion, I wish that I had the time and ability to share all that I've learned on the subject of design, but I made it clear that I wouldn't be counting beans. If you are a skeptic, then I implore you to research these opposing views. I believe that all people are blessed to know instinctively of God's existence and are without an excuse and those who remain in denial of God are merely fooling themselves. Regardless of our mystical inclinations, we cannot have it both ways. Some will try to mix and match their thoughts on God, but in the end you either believe in the one true God or you don't. I've expressed the idea to many people that having a belief in design should be as easy as finding something green in the Pacific Northwest, but to truly know God takes a bit more investigating. If you are an atheist, then this won't apply to you, but for the rest of us, it should be noted that science will not make God appear in all his glory, but it is part of his plan for us to use science to better understand him.

God gave us a road map—science of discovery is only one part. There is the revealed Word, prophecies, and miracles. There is the incarnation, the fulfillment of the messianic prophecies that are concluded with the death and resurrection. There are gifts that are present in our every breath. You can know God. You can move from belief to conviction. Take the time to seek, and you will find what you are looking for. Along the way, if you are true to yourself, you will discard the irrelevant in lieu of the greatest gift of all: grace!

Chapter 11

Learning to Read

It is the duty of every cultured man or woman to read sympathetically the scriptures of the world. If we are to respect others' religions as we would have them respect our own, a friendly study of the world's religions is a sacred duty.

Gandhi

Part 1: Words of Wisdom

Most people know how to read. If you don't, then somebody is reading this to you and hopefully you can overcome your obstacle. For the rest of us, we can pick and choose what we want to read, and the choices seem endless. If you read sleazy romance novels, you can learn diabolical ways to betray your loved ones and thwart your archenemy. If you read the tabloids, you can fill your head with useless gossip about people you'll never know. If you read *Modern Science,* you will be updated on the latest technologies, and you might find yourself awestruck in the human ability to construct. If you read *Newsweek,* you will be updated on the latest slimeball Republican, whereas if you read the Limbaugh Letter, you'll be updated on the latest slimeball Democrat. The list goes on and on, and we all want information about what interests us.

If you read for about an hour a day, then you read much more than the average American. If you read an hour a day about anything to do with history, then you moved into a new echelon. If you read more than an hour a day on the topic of theology and you're not in the business of teaching theology or in the ministries, then you are truly a rarity. There is a problem with a lack of reading, and it is even more troubling when we discover what many Americans are reading. Great pleasure can be found in reading a novel, and most of the classics convey a moral that can be useful in everyday life. We quote these books and their morals constantly, even though we are often hard pressed to remember where they originated. This occurrence is most prevalent in biblical verses, because even if a person has never read the Bible, they will quote it at some point in their life.

"The meek shall inherit the earth."
"You are the salt of the earth."
"You are the light of the world."
"Turn the other cheek."
"Love your neighbors."
"Love your enemies."
"Where your treasure is, there your heart will be also."
"Do not judge or you too will be judged."
"For wide is the gate and broad is the road that leads to destruction."

Here we have a few verses taken from one sermon recorded in the book of Matthew. They were spoken by Jesus in the Sermon on the Mount. While quoting these verses, we often butcher them, but we have all heard a variation of most. In the Bible, however, they are not butchered and remain in context. Most people have heard these words, but some have little understanding as to their true meaning. They simply interpret them in their own way. If they had taken the time to read and understand these passages, then they might find that they have great value.

One of the most overused phrases in our culture today is applied when a person finds himself in a tricky spot over something they said: "I was taken out of context." This can save you much hardship from the masses, but the people who actually take the time to read the transcript will remain aware of the true meaning behind your words. If you do not take the time to research the transcript, then you are left to believe the person or not, based on their personal merits. People are sly, and they require an investigation. Even if you read and investigate a subject, you may still be puzzled, and if so, read around the subject and get several points of view from people whom you find trustworthy and who have your best interest at heart. At that point, while using the reason and logic that you are endowed with, a conclusion may be found.

A troubling situation can occur when people in any culture become lethargic and begin to rely on others to perform their inquiries for them. Their skills of logic and reason become dull, and when a soiled thought or idea is presented to them, they are easily sold. Young Mormon missionaries believe that the Church of Latter-Day Saints is a traditional Christian church, or at least a denomination of the Christian Church. Nothing could be further from the truth, but they still believe it. If a young Mormon on his mission took the time to investigate church history and the writings of his own Mormon founders, he would find many contradictions in the core tenants of the two books currently in his backpack.

The same could be said about a person (*Nancy Pelosi*) who claims to be a Catholic but champions a woman's right to kill. Or a person (*Nancy Pelosi*) who claims to be a Catholic but is an advocate for gay rights. That person (*Nancy Pelosi*) would be living a contradictory life far removed from her stated beliefs. This person (*Nancy Pelosi*) probably wants universal health care so she can get a deal on the sleeping pills she must need to sleep at night. The logical and reasonable thing for this person (*Nancy Pelosi*) to do is to stop relying on the age-old political excuse, "I can't let my personal beliefs get in the way of what is constitutional" and come down from the pedestal of power and help others move away from their destructive lifestyles. Sorry Nancy, God isn't going to buy the separation of church and state excuse when the time comes. I know that I promised not to get too personal, but our speaker isn't speaking for me, and she apparently isn't the voice of the Catholic Church either.

Part 2: Tell Me What You Know

My good friend Jeff West always said, "Don't tell me what you feel, tell me what you know." He purposely avoiding saying that to me, because he knew he would be in for a long discussion. Some pretend to be an authority on subjects that are completely beyond their understanding. Rosie O'Donnell slams Christians with breakfast but shows little understanding of the Christian doctrine. It would easy to conclude that she has never read the Bible, and if so, it was probably in part and she most assuredly never took the time to truly understand the message or seek out the understanding from others who do know. In other words, she knows just enough to be dangerous but far too little to actually understand.

The same can be said about a plethora of subjects and the people who claim to be experts with little or no investigation. You've heard it said that "Defending yourself in a court of law is the equivalent of performing brain surgery on yourself." Basically, that is true, simply because lawyers talk in a coded language to insure that they will be needed to decipher the code whenever a person's freedom or wealth is at stake. Watching *LA Law* is not going to make you a great defense lawyer. It may give you a fictional sample of the lingo, but you'll still get convicted while defending yourself. When it comes to theology or philosophy, it gets worse, especially in today's culture when there appears to be no wrong answer. I could throw some apologetics your way, but it is best left to the experts, as I am not C. S. Lewis or Ravi Zacharias. If I pretended to be, then I would be guilty of expressing feelings over substance. In a later chapter, I will add more substance, but it will be limited to what I know, and I'll leave my feelings at the door.

Part 3: Little Steps

If you fall into one of the categories that I mentioned before and reading is not a priority to you, then I suggest you start small. Read something of interest that only begins to challenge you. Everybody has a subject or two that interests them but that they have, for one reason or another, abandoned. We all have the time; it is merely a matter of priority. An interesting thing happens when you begin to read about a subject of interest: generally, you want to know more. This explains why a Civil War buff has a bookshelf littered with books on war. He might have started out interested in only the Civil War, but that led to a desire to know about other wars. Eventually, he will read opposing views on different wars and come to a logical and reasonable conclusion. If you rely on the History Channel to inform you about a particular war, you will fool many, but not this guy. He knows his stuff and he's heard the arguments from every angle. Basically, he did his homework and you watched a television summary.

More books have been written on theology and philosophy than any other subject, and ironically, they are for the most part ignored in today's culture. It would seem to an outsider, looking in, that the top priority to an American reader is smut. I put pornography, tabloids, gossip, romance novels, and smear-merchant journalism all under the heading of smut. First, we need to simply read more to protect our language and to enhance our ability to communicate. Secondly, we need to read more literature of value. I have zero desire to make any conclusions for you, therefore, if you wish to believe that aliens from another planet killed JFK, then God bless you. If, on the other hand, you wish to convey that idea to me, then you better have more than a feeling to back it up.

Most people never read the Constitution, but we all say at one time or another that something that disturbs us is unconstitutional. Most people know very little about Ronald Reagan, but our opinions are loud and clear in opposing positions. Likewise, we all have an opinion on God. It may be short and sweet: "I believe in God" or it may be short and abrupt: "There is no God," but the opinion is there. You could be one of many with a long and vague opinion, which I find useless and tiresome as I prefer the short and graceful opinion when the topic is salvation and the long and detailed version when describing how a person reached their final decision.

In conclusion, I have always found it interesting that so many people who claim to have a belief in a deity never take the time to investigate what he might be trying to tell them. We may be spoken to in many ways other than the written word, but to know what is truly revealed and to be a conveyor of the words; we need to read the words. Saying kind words and expressing your humility is a great way to show that God is an important part of your life; for many, seeing the humility in another is all that is needed. They will see the changes that God has made in others, and they want to be part of the club. Once part of the club, it is important to learn the rules of the club and to teach others. At some point, we need to examine what we believe and why we believe it, and reading is an essential part. It could be the very reason that building blocks for toddlers have letters on them.

Just a Thought #8

Watching the History Channel or Discovery will not make you an informed individual. Even if the presentation has a collaboration of many voices with opposing points of view, there is only one director. That director is in charge of final editing, and he will certainly lean the final copy in his direction. In some cases, a director will flat out lie to you or omit information that makes the presentation laughable. *Banned from the Bible* is a perfect example. The producers and director of this series have an entirely secular agenda and will deceive anyone who doesn't take the time to investigate their absurd conclusions.

Chapter 12

We're the Kids in America

All schools and colleges have two great functions: to confer and conceal valuable knowledge. The theological knowledge which they conceal cannot justly be regarded as less valuable than that which they reveal. That is, when a man is buying a basket of strawberries, it can profit him to know that the bottom half is rotten.

Mark Twain

Part 1: School Days

In 1976, I was in the sixth grade and I had an obnoxious friend named Troy Don. He was the ultimate class clown; he was always in trouble but forever humorous. Everybody loved him, and that oversized head on his skinny frame only added to his humor. The teachers and administrators who were forced to discipline him seemed to do so with hidden smiles because they too were taken in by his playful nature. Our sixth-grade teacher, Mr. Briggs, was a stern guy, and he wasn't yet shackled or hindered with the politically correct notions that today's teachers must endure. One particular day, Troy was really pushing Mr. Briggs's buttons. All through the morning, Troy was disrupting class with humorous outbursts that were causing the veins to pop out on Mr.

Briggs's forehead. When it came time for lunch, as was the tradition at Mira Monte Elementary, Mr. Briggs walked us to the cafeteria line. We were not a minute into the cafeteria when Troy started his usual ruckus of blathering shenanigans. It was then that Mr. Briggs finally said with a sigh, "You really think you're something special don't you, Troy?"

To which Troy replied (as only he could), "I'm not only something special, Mr. Briggs, I'm perfect."

At that point, there may have been a nanosecond delay before Mr. Briggs's violent response, but I can't remember one. What I do remember is what he said and those present to hear it. In front of the entire class, the principal (who just happened to be behind the counter getting his own lunch) and anyone within a hundred-foot radius, he screamed, "There was only one perfect man and that was Jesus Christ, and you, Troy, are not Jesus Christ!" There was no response from Troy, or anyone else for that matter. I think the principal merely nodded in agreement and continued scooping navy beans on his plate to go along with his Salisbury steak. No one jotted down notes, nobody complained; it was just over. Troy moved away a year later and Mr. Briggs continued teaching for many years. Looking back, I realize that the sheer volume of his voice would have subjected him to suspension and ridicule if it were to have happened today. What he actually said would have cost him his job and any hope of finding another in the field of academia.

Mr. Briggs had simply stated his belief with zero apologies to those around him. Today, the educational climate has changed drastically and when we are not allowed to teach children what we believe, we are surely shortchanging them. If you read the thoughts on education from our forefathers, you will find that they believed that children should learn religion and morals first and everything else second. If we do not learn the religious beliefs of those trying to instruct us and compare those with other beliefs, then the authority figure loses his impact. Leaving the moral virtues and their origin out of the classroom will produce children who will become creatures of the secular world. Basically, they will only hear one side of the story (and the less important one at that).

They might become great achievers and world shakers, but items of true importance will be lost on them.

Bill gates is under the belief that religion is simply not an efficient way to spend our cherished time and that there are many other worthwhile things that we can and should be doing on any given Sunday.

Sadly, that pretty much sums up the thinking of a large portion of American culture today. Not only do many see God as unobtainable and undesirable, but they also see him as inefficient to their busy schedules.

Kids in the public school system do learn religion, but it is the religion of secularism. The course is required curriculum from preschool right up through their college graduation. They are entrenched with ideas of pluralism, multiculturalism, and of course, naturalism. The purveyors of these ideas are either too cowardly to inform their students of the traditional alternative or have become true believers themselves. The true believers of skepticism are on the rise and they're digging in. Teachers are for the most part liberal; they spend eighteen years being bombarded with a particular ideology and then after a summer playing in the sun, are quickly thrown into a group of people (mainly college professors) who have never left the sanctimonious classroom. These college professors balk at the private sector, which generally pays their salaries; they ridicule the traditional system and profess their ideology as fact-based to developing minds.

After four or more years of being enlightened to the progressive mindset, it becomes a difficult task shaking the state ideology. For teachers, this task becomes an even larger obstacle because they (like their idols at the college lecterns) never leave the classroom. Even if teacher does possess a good theology and sees through the hypocrisy, he would be forced to keep his mouth shut and his eyes closed if they hope to remain gainfully employed. The NEA is a disgrace; it will squash free speech at every turn, while developing new teaching robots who have long since forgotten to think for themselves. These robotic foot soldiers for the progressive movement are at liberty to engage in politically correct blather while oppressing young minds and any form of truth they might have obtained. Once a teacher or college professor has achieved tenure, they can crank up the fire on his lies and rhetoric without fear of consequence—and if a problem does arise, they has the ACLU to protect them free of charge.

It is well documented that the public school system is crammed full of hypocrites. If that is a surprise to you, then you are either in school or you are teaching school. To just about everyone else above the age of forty, their insincerity is as transparent as an elephant trying to disguise himself as one of the Olsen twins.

Nowhere is their display of sanctimony more on display than in matters of faith. They want our children to take giant leaps of faith on age-old theories and abandon our valued traditions. Most teaching professionals believe that they have a moral obligation to defend the politically correct. The main focus of a teaching professional is the elimination of oppression toward any student; and in doing so, they need to oppress ideas. If one idea is to be considered in the classroom, then they must bring all ideas to the table; therefore it was at once decided to create a state ideology and abandon all others. The establishment could never allow opposing ideas that do not coincide with their own, because this would run counterintuitive to their cause. State run institutions have their own ideology, bordering on a religion that they refuse to share with opposing viewpoints. Even if the course is theology, the main tenets of each religion will be rendered as irrelevant. This will be done to either deny a particular faith or to omit it altogether. Eventually, they will try to pilot any wayward thoughts back to the established state religion of naturalism. They have little choice.

If you are under thirty, then you probably think that evolution holds most of the answers about your existence. If your parents never taught you otherwise, what are you to think? Liberal lawmakers are currently working on a bill that would make it mandatory that your child starts his public education at three. They want to avoid the annoying possibility that a parent might implant an idea of a creator in a young developing mind before the establishment gets their filthy hands on them. Before a young adult receives their college degree, they will have spent twenty plus years being fed one side of a story and many will be indoctrinated to the point of no return. I have had many conversations with the recently graduated, and although they will use multi-syllable words in an attempt to project their message, it will usually be left to vague theories and it will lack a point. When the only common denominator in a large group of individuals is that truth is relative, we have a huge problem brewing. This backward ideology takes truth out of the hands of the Creator and puts it directly into the unworthy hands of the destroyer.

The roots of this movement can be traced back to centuries past, but in America, the movement is a little behind the curve. We didn't board the secular train at full force until the thirties, and that explains why we are not as advanced in debauchery as other industrialized nations. In Europe, there are few hindrances on behavior, and their rapid decay in morality tells the tale. In America, we mostly remain a nation of believers, but for how long? We need to tear down the public education system, as it has become a monster—and monsters, as you may remember from your childhood fears, need to be destroyed.

If it is financially possible, send your kids to a private school. *Private* is a hated term for a secular progressive and you can use this as an incentive. The NEA has little if any control over the curriculum in a private school and they hate losing control. The teachers at a private school will be at liberty to teach all points of view and profess what they believe to be preposterous and what they hold dear to them.

If you cannot afford a private school, then home school. You will be under the guidance of the NEA, but you will have much more control and you will be avoiding the perpetrators of fallacy. If you can't find the time to home school, then find a friend or relative who can. You might be surprised what a person will do for a free lunch. If you need to wait until your child is old enough to stay home alone, then that is the right time to start home schooling. Every time a child leaves the public school system, it sends a message to the NEA: "We are tired of swallowing their medicine." If you fear that the lack of social skills might hinder your child's development, involve them in other activities with other kids.

Try setting up a neighborhood home schooling schedule where there are many like-minded parents who can share the burden of teaching and looking after the kids. That would solve time restraints and the social skills issue at the same time.

Finally, don't be asleep at the wheel. Take the time to get involved locally and help those in positions of power to promote the school voucher system. When you see curriculum that is contrary to rational thought, speak out. If the history that is being taught is unrecognizable from what you learned in school, ask why. If this battle for the minds of our children is lost, then we will only have ourselves to blame. If we remain apathetic in regards to education, then we are doomed to a world of perversion, blasphemy, and zero accountability.

Secular progressive teachers are not going to give up this fight until they are forced into a reverse education machine. One doesn't exist so we must continue to play the numbers game. Hopefully, we will someday live in a country where children are exposed to opposing views on every subject. Where good teachers are not gagged, where a theory will be taught as a mere theory, where absurdities will be quickly pointed out, and where Mr. Briggs would remain gainfully employed. These scoundrels want the minds and souls of our children in order to push their secular agenda. The more people on the highway to hell, the less guilt will be felt by those in the driver's seat.

This is a fight we can and must win, but we need a real hero to step to the forefront like a modern day Vince Lombardi to rally the troops or a brave individual who is willing to dedicate his life to exposing the NEA for who they truly are. Either way, we must shed our lazy, apathetic ways and step to the forefront. Try making loud, obnoxious noises. Naturalistic protesters do it every day and they don't even have a logical reason.

Just a Thought #9

Always, always, always remember that your children are going to believe what you tell them. (At least until they learn that you are not as reliable a source as they once thought.) If you enchant your children with mystical idealism when they are young, then they will most likely grow to have a mystical thought process. Allowing your children to role play in the fantasy world is one thing, but the failure to explain the difference between fantasy and reality might actually produce more Scientologists. And you thought college was expensive!

Part 2: The Questionnaire

To find the thought process of a certain group of individuals, you need to ask them the same questions. This is why surveying has become a full-time job for marketing firms and political advocates. I wanted to find out what is the prevailing thought process in regards to theology among college students from varying backgrounds and beliefs. I compiled a short list of questions and my findings were just as I had thought they would be: "maddening." After obtaining basic information about age, background, and professed religion, I asked the following questions.

(I will first show you the questionnaire and how I would have answered it, and then I'll follow up with my findings.)

Do you believe in God?   Y or N
My answer: Y

Do you believe the nature of man is good or bad? Please explain.

My answer
Bad.

Having the humility to let the light of truth shine on my personal life has shown my nature to be bad. It is only when I weigh myself against others that I tend to see myself as good. Therefore, if compared to mankind as it was originally intended to be I still find myself bad then it must be in our nature. Civilizations have always gone from bad to worse as portrayed in every history book. They can be revived for a period but eventually they will fall, just as Adam fell and every man who followed: It is uniquely in our nature.

Do you believe the universe is infinite or finite? Please explain.

My answer:
Finite.

I believe that science and reason leads one to believe that the universe had a beginning from a source separate from the universe. Therefore it would make logical sense that the Creator could at any time end the universe. The God I believe in has revealed that he will end this universe and create a new one. Science sheds light on this belief in the mere fact that our universe will decay to a point of no longer being able to sustain life. The Bible has laid claim to God as being the alpha and the omega, both the beginning and the end.

Do you believe truth is relative? Please explain.

My answer:
No.

Perception of the truth can vary depending on viewpoint, but *truth* remains constant. Two things cannot occupy the same place at the same time and that includes opposing truths. For something to be true, it cannot share space with a falsehood. The human mind can make it appear as if truth can be relative, but in the end, the problem is with the mind not the truth.

Do you believe in hell? Y or N
My answer: Y

Do you believe that all faiths lend a hand in finding ultimate truth? Please explain.

My answer:
No.

They might have a hint of the truth, but to find ultimate truth, we must find the one true God because he is the ultimate truth. If a faith needs to be gutted to make it fit with other faiths, then the whole pluralistic idea loses validity. Contrasting opinions can only be welded together with compromise. I refuse to believe in a compromising God.

Do you believe that religion is counterproductive to society? Please explain.

My answer:

It depends on the religion.

If we are to subscribe to the mystical Eastern thought process of treating a rock as you would treat your brother, then society would be greatly affected. We would need to wait for a tree to fall before harvesting it and most of us would be living in caves. We would be cold nudists because we would need to wait until the natural death of animals and plant life in order to be clothed. If, on the other hand, you believe in a God who has revealed to you that you are exalted over plant life and animals and has left you with a record of how to live correctly (both inherited and in his Word) then religion can be very productive in society. Perversions of any religion can be counterproductive, and this perversion can be found in every world view, which often leads to great atrocities.

What is your overall world view in regards to religion or philosophy? Please explain.

My answer:

The full answer to this question will be found in a later chapter.

Part 3: The Findings

I surveyed well over a hundred college students between the ages of eighteen and thirty and I asked them the same questions that I answered above. In order to display my findings, we must first categorize the subjects to have a better understanding of their answers. Twelve percent claimed a belief in Eastern thought of one kind or another. Six percent claimed to be atheist. Eight percent believed in altered or borrowed faiths such as Islam or Mormonism, and seventy-four percent claimed to be Christian. Secondly, we must determine the level of their held belief. Are they devout in their beliefs or moderately devout? This leaves us eight categories of respondents to examine. After we examine the findings, I'll amuse you with some of the crazy answers as well as some of the more thought-provoking ones.

Group #1: The Devout Eastern Thinker

This group is hard to pin down. A Western modification to their original belief has persuaded many to abandon some of the core tenets of their faith. They are mostly in agreement about life being an illusion. They are also in agreement about reincarnation and most practice meditation. They hate any idea about hell and hold in contempt those who do believe in hell. The relativity of truth is of no concern to the majority of this group, because it has no effect on their illusion. They believe that religion has an effect on their illusory perceptions and usually in a bad way. Peace through meditation is at the core of what they consider virtuous, and this and only this can bring about a change to the cycle of reincarnation. The universe is infinite to this group inasmuch as if people continue to imagine it exists then it will. Overall, this group puts all their apples in one basket, and if any part of the basket tears, then the apples will come crashing down. If our very existence is proved to be more than an illusion, then this group is left to rethink their entire belief system. Without reincarnation, there is little chance of reaching the next level (unless they have already achieved pure enlightenment, which might be problematic when trying to explain their next headache).

Group #2: The Moderate Eastern Thinker

In each of these "moderate" categories, I will quickly and briefly give you their mindset.

This group is deeply confused. The majority of the group believes in reincarnation, but few practice meditation. They are split on having many gods or in all things being God. They hate the idea of hell and are staunch believers in the idea that truth is relative. This group was all over the map in areas of human nature and the life of the universe. Basically, they really didn't know what to believe.

Group #3: The Devout Atheist

This group was hard to obtain information from. They obviously have an aversion towards God, but they were unwilling to participate in most questions. They appeared more ready to fall on the sword than to discuss any matter beyond the proclamation of there being no God. Though I only talked to a few (atheists are harder to find than you might think), there was one guy who was willing to expound upon his feelings more than the others. I cannot say he speaks for all atheists, but I have a feeling that his insight will be shared with many other likeminded individuals. He spoke openly about the personal disappointments he had experienced in life. He also expressed the sorrow for others that he had seen suffering, both personally and across the globe. He said that he refused to believe in a God that would allow children to suffer and die from starvation or disease. He also held a strong belief that wars that had been waged throughout the centuries were a result of man's need to be correct in the arena of religion, and without religion, there would be nothing to fight and die for. In the end, it was the lack of empirical knowledge of God that was his loophole. If God exists, then why not make it known to all?

Answers to his questions can be long and drawn out, and are best left to a professional, but I can say this: people do not need religion to have a reason to fight wars; we fight over drugs, money, and power all the time. In a quick response to empirical knowledge, it basically comes down to faith and trust. Just as you could never force anyone to love you, God chose to give you the ability to love and he desires real love. Basically, we are not robots; we are created beings in God's image and have the ability to give love freely which is the only kind worth having.

Group #4: The Moderate Atheist

This group would like to describe themselves as agnostic, but that permits way too much wiggle room for me. They might profess that they don't really know whether a god exists or not, but they have turned away from their search and in doing so have earned the title of an atheist. You might find a set of keys a couple of days after you have stopped looking for them, but God might be harder to find by surprise for those who have stopped seeking him. This group seemed happier than the devout atheist and for obvious reasons. Though once again, I only spoke to a few, they seemed more consumed by earthly rewards and held very hedonistic tendencies that seemed to be holding their search at bay. Basically, they had never given the idea of God much thought and they were far too busy in their day-to-day lives to seek knowledge of a God who to them, appears unobtainable. By the way, I think that this group is much larger then it appears. If you really break it down, there are many people who give lip service to God but who really don't know Him. It is as if knowing God will somehow disrupt their lives and all the fringe benefits of living. It isn't until a person realizes that they truly have nothing without God, that they are willing to part from whatever form of idolatry possesses them.

Group #5: The Devout (Altered or Borrowed Believer)

It would take a long time to divide these believers into their different world views based on each religion. Therefore, we will look at what they hold in common. Whether it is Joseph Smith of the Mormon faith, Charles Taze Russell of the Jehovah's Witnesses, or Muhammad of Islam, this group loves their founders. Their founders are worshipped to a degree, and their teaching is considered sacred. The founders of these borrowed faiths have trumped what has been previously written in the Bible and nullified the original meaning. This group is having trouble with college life, as they seem to be getting just enough contrary information to raise doubt about their faith. Unfortunately, this group doesn't know much about church history and has not been schooled on the origin scripture, so they are ill informed to expand on their beliefs. They are quick to defend their faith with well-rehearsed arguments, but they can add little more to the argument other than their belief that the Bible was misinterpreted and that their particular founder was chosen to set the record straight.

Group #6: The Moderate (Altered or Borrowed Believer)

This group fit into college life much better than their devout counterparts. They hold dear to their hearts that truth is relative and that whatever they believe has zero bearing on what is true for another. Their faith is more of a heritage than that of a compass. It appears that their religion has roots in their upbringing but little bearing on their future. They did profess a belief in God or many gods, but had a hard time describing him or them. They had a quick and shallow response to questions about their faith, in that basically, it was considered personal. In all, I spoke to a little more than twenty people in these two altered faith categories. Most were Mormons and a couple of Jehovah's Witnesses, but of all the Muslims I spoke with, not one was placed into the moderate group. That's odd!

Group #7: The Devout Christian

This group was extremely divided. I wish that I could say that they all knew their theology, but I can't. Thirty percent answered the questions in a similar fashion as I answered them above, but the remaining 70 percent had varying thoughts. They were, however, joined at the hip in certain areas. They all believed in God, but most didn't believe that it was their place to point out what was wrong for another. Amazingly, they had pluralistic beliefs that made them shy away from concluding that their faith held the keys to ultimate truth. Truth for this 70 percent was for the individual and they found my response to the questions distasteful and narrow-minded. The fact that God is narrow-minded in areas of morality seems lost to them. I would love to commit this portion of the group to the moderate Christians, but I can't honestly label them. They need to do that for themselves.

It quickly became apparent to me that calling yourself "devout" doesn't necessarily make you devout. Fair amounts of the 70 percent do not believe in hell even though their faith's namesake—Christ himself—spoke more about hell than anyone else in the Bible. When analyzing this 70 percent of respondents, it is clear that they were never taught the meat of their religion. If they had been taught the core tenets, they must have been asleep at the wheel. There are many Christian ministers across the country that spend their Sundays projecting a well-orchestrated and cleverly displayed morality. There is nothing wrong with a good moral, but the words that God has revealed should never be sugar coated. Pastors and parents should be ashamed that a young adult has little to offer in the way of defense for their faith. If a young Christian is afraid to make waves, then what does that say for Jesus? He made tremendous waves. Not all Christians are meant to be apologists for the church, but they should at least be able to give an account for why they believe and make zero apologies for it. The book that they call holy, demands that an account be at the ready.

Group #8: The Moderate Christian

This group is linked directly with the 70 percent of confused, self-proclaimed, devout Christians. The only true distinction is in the degree of their confusion. This group wasn't asleep during services, because most of them rarely attended in the first place. They hold little understanding of the Christian faith and had no misgivings about the idea that it is none of their business to reach out to others. They proclaimed their Christianity as more of a birthright than an actual relationship with God. Few believed in hell, and most believed that if there were a hell, they surely didn't belong there. They are quick to respond that it is the individual who decides morality and that ultimate truth can be found in varying ways. I must add that I find it hard to believe that there can be a moderate Christian. If you don't have a pilot's license and you've never been on an airplane or studied aviation, then you will be hard-pressed to convince others that you are a pilot.

I talked with several interesting people during this study and received varying responses. I was most intrigued by a few answers that were so removed from reality that I need to share a few.

One student whose name will be withheld actually believes that everybody has one particular part of the puzzle. When combined with the other parts from all others, both living and dead, it will eventually lead us to an ultimate truth and free us from our hardship. The puzzle parts of the dead are to be channeled by living family members when the puzzle is near completion.

Another student believed that hell is a place where you go to live the life that you have chosen here on earth, and it doesn't need to be a bad thing. All people end up in hell, but it will be an exact depiction of how you live your life here on earth. If you spend all your time worshipping God, then you will receive a sort of hell that is an eternal church service. If, on the other hand, you choose to hang out at a bar drinking, then that will be your eternal destination. This student believed in living a well-balanced life so he can spend eternity never being bored. Personally, I think this guy needs to learn the meaning of the word *hell*.

Finally, I had one student who couldn't be included in my study. She would have required her own category. This gal believed in naturalism to a newfound degree and in a reverse manner. She believes that since we originated from simpler organisms, they are to be worshipped as gods. The simpler the species, the closer they are to God. She believes that humans are the lowest of life forms, proven by their ability to destroy. Plant life is held in a higher spectrum than the animal kingdom because they have no ability to hunt and eat other life forms. This idea probably came to her during a drug-induced hallucination. If not, she should probably pretend that it did.

In conclusion, it can be said without reservation that most young adults in American academia are confused and have little idea what to believe. They hold truth as being relative as their most common ground. Regardless of their belief, most are not willing to defend their faith out of fear of being labeled as oppressive. With few exceptions, life's bigger questions are not being asked. The students seem well occupied with the reasoning of the secular world and are not too entrenched in any belief system. Some of the devout understand their personal faith, but most have never really expanded deeply into the subject. Most of the questions were foreign to them and required explanation prior to their answering. It is troubling when a college student has made it to their level of education and has never been challenged with real philosophical questions. Somebody is not doing their job.

Children should be well armed to answer the absurd claims that will await them in any level of education. Failing to teach your child about truth and where it comes from will be leaving their formative brains in the hands of professional charlatans. The only way to stop these transmitters of fallacy is to outnumber them and halt their exploitation. When enough logical, thinking students avoid this deluge of secularism and work to become teachers themselves, the tide will turn. Unfortunately, the logical, thinking student can only learn to think correctly away from the public educational system. That is why it is crucial that we no longer remain apathetic as this is a fight worth waging.

Chapter 13

Common Sense

Part 1: In Gus we Trust

One of my favorite films is *Lonesome Dove,* filmed in 1989. It is a story of two retired Texas Rangers who decide to leave the border town of Lonesome Dove in Texas for the pristine countryside of Montana. Filmed in a miniseries format, the story is long but beautifully portrayed. The northern move is hard, and the characters face many obstacles that keep the viewer's attention throughout. The two main characters are Augustus McCrae (played by Robert Duvall) and his partner Woodrow Call (played by Tommy Lee Jones). These men appear as polar opposites with a single exception: McCrea is a playboy who enjoys gambling, women, and alcohol, while Call is a dutiful taskmaster who focuses on working the ranch and keeping others in line. In all great literature, partners have a common thread that holds them together. Whether it is a common goal or a simple world view, they must develop to the notion that they are united for a purpose or the story would unravel. McCrea and Call had a common purpose of relocating, but McCrea was not as passionate about the move north as Call; he would have been satisfied to live out the remainder of his days in Lonesome Dove. While being polar opposites, the two are bound together by the love for one another (that is apparent throughout the film) and the noble ability to differentiate between what made sense and what didn't. The word "sense" is used at every turn as the pair watch with nodding heads when a hand or two shows a lack thereof.

McCrea: "That don't make a lick of sense, Woodrow."

Call: "No, I reckon it don't."

Above all else, we are left with the idea that these are two completely different people who are joined together with wisdom in a similar manner. They trusted each other because they knew that the characteristics they shared were far greater attributes then their opposing lifestyles that might have otherwise made them bitter enemies. Common sense, by its very definition, does not lend itself to contrasting ideologies; it is this *sense* that, with practical use, we can forever be united, while leaving mythology behind.

Part 2: Thomas Paine

In 1776, Americans declared their independence from Great Britain. Interestingly enough, it was the same year that Thomas Paine penned the pamphlet "Common Sense." which was given to colonists who were undecided as to the declaration. Paine used the Bible to make his arguments against British rule, monarchy, and the hereditary succession while instituting an approach that could be seen by colonists as pure common sense. Looking over the famous quotes contained in this pamphlet, it is easy to see why it had an enormous impact on the early Americans who still held tight to their core beliefs and their reliability on what made sense.

Here are some quotes from Thomas Paine's "Common Sense." They ring as true today as they did 233 years ago.

"Some writers have so confounded society with government, as to leave little or no distinction between them; whereas they are not only different, but have different origins."

"A long habit of not thinking a thing wrong gives it a superficial appearance of being right, and raises at first a formidable outcry in defense of custom."

"In the early stages of the world, according to scripture chronology, there were no kings; the consequence of which was, there were no wars; it is the pride of kings which throws mankind into confusion."

"Government by kings was first introduced into the world by Heathens, from whom the children of Israel copied the custom. It was the most preposterous invention the Devil ever set on foot for the promotion of idolatry."

"But where, say some, is the King of America? I'll tell you, friend, he reigns above, and doth not make havoc of mankind like the Royal Brute of Great Britain...so far as we approve of monarchy, that in America the law is king."

"Have every opportunity and every encouragement before us, to form the noblest purest constitution on the face of the earth. We have it in our power to begin the world over again. A situation similar to the present, hath not happened since the days of Noah until now. The birthday of a new world is at hand, and a race of men, perhaps as numerous as all Europe contains, are to receive their portion of freedom from the event of a few months."

"Time makes more converts then reason."

"I offer nothing more than simple facts, plain arguments, and common sense."

This is powerful stuff and it is sadly lost in American culture today. Paine was not only opposed to a monarchy system; he found it to be the greatest tool used by the devil himself to bring upheaval upon mankind. If it can be said that all men are flawed, then it can be conceded that all human kings are flawed as well. Absolute power leads to a prideful stance of the one bestowed of power and the destruction of liberty to all others. Paine used the biblical idea that we are created equal and that no one person is to negate our freedom. In using the argument of custom,

Paine cleverly illustrated the notion that people will eventually be lulled into a state of bondage with time being the conqueror.

In his pamphlet, Thomas Paine used what traditions and virtues were held in common of most colonists to punctuate his point. Using the Bible to illustrate the ideology that would become our Founding Fathers' stronghold was ingenious. People are united by what they hold in common and in what makes sense in each varying situation. Referring to a higher power for his words of wisdom left believers (of which there were many) nowhere to logically hide. It is not a great mystery that these biblically inspired words, written in a time of revolution, have been neglected and for the most part forgotten. Time is the culprit and power is its companion. Today, the government has obtained massive power; the representatives are tending to their own desires while neglecting ambitiously blind people who assisted them to their lofty position. As a country, we are moving toward a form of monarchy that must be reversed to form a nation with people united in a common goal that Paine so passionately spoke of.

Unfortunately, to become united as a nation, we need to hold common beliefs and traditions that have been rapidly eroding throughout the last few decades. Paine looked to America's King as being the King from above: the King of Kings in which to build our nation. The new world that he spoke of was strong and held its head high for many generations only to see it slowly decay from within; with our severed ties of faith and virtues, we are sure to slide quickly and gently into that good night.

Even to the non-believer or the mystics, it should be apparent that to survive as a nation, we must hold true to the traditions and values that once bond us together and made us whole. There is no greater attribute to the forming of our nation then the common held belief in the God of the Bible; without which, Thomas Paine's words would have made little if any impact and the bright, shiny city on the hill would probably be vacation land for Nazi Germany.

Part 3: Common Threads

In more modern and practical terms, we cannot equate common sense with relativism; inasmuch as it doesn't make sense, it is also an oxymoron. I guess everybody has a lick of sense (as Augustus McCrea might say) but which, if any, of these senses do we currently hold in common with all other Americans? Not too many, and that is our problem! While an argument could be made that if the vast majority of colonists were Hindus and Paine used that commonality to unite the people toward independence the results may have, at first, been similar, but the results of retaining our freedom in light of the oppressing world would be in stark contrast to what history reveals. Christianity was our former commonalty, and the Bible was used as a reference point in the formation of our nation, our government, and all who sought our shores. Christianity has been perverted, watered down, and used as an iron fist in many countries, including our own. However, the core tenets that could never be perverted and that were once used to inspire the forming of our nation have since been ripped from our grasp and ridiculed as irrelevant.

As an American, you are currently at liberty to say that you believe Christianity is not only false, but detrimental to our society. In being an American, I am also at liberty to say that you are wrong, and history is my wingman. We can lock heads all day long with the varying events throughout American history, but in the end, we will require the knowledge that people come together through a common thought process—and they slip apart as quickly as they forget that they once shared a likeness in that thought. Americans once assimilated to the newfound culture that flourished between our shores. We were a proud group of patriotic Christians, and while flawed in many ways, we overcame many self-made obstacles to become prosperous, generous, and a beacon of hope throughout the world. If we are to lose our most common thread that binds us, then what will we become as a nation? If we ban cars from the car show, we no longer have a car show. If we ridicule and persecute Christians at every turn in a nation held together by the commonalities of our Christian founders, we will no longer have a nation.

Regardless of your beliefs, keep this in mind: you may not like oranges, but you probably won't ban them or ridicule them if you own an Orange Julius stand at the mall. Oranges are the main ingredient that keeps your stand thriving, and to remove them would lead to sure failure. There are those among us in positions of power who wish to tear down this country and start fresh with age-old ideologies that probably won't seem revolutionary to readers of Thomas Paine. These proprietors of a new nation will wish to return to tried and failed government systems while recognizing the need to eradicate the main ingredient of the prior; Christianity!

If you hold America with any level of esteem, then it would only make common sense to defend her traditions, her values, and her faith-based world view. To do otherwise would render us as a separated people, impotent, and useless in the generations to come.

Chapter 14

Contemporary Americana

Part 1: A Sad State of Affairs

Morality is of the highest importance—but for us, not for God.

Albert Einstein

God gave man free will, and evil ensued. America gave its people free enterprise, and greed and corruption ensued. Both free will and free enterprise are good things; it is the people awarded those gifts who are corrupt. There are countless social ills to count in America today, and sometimes watching the evening news can make me want to vomit. Billy Graham once said that America asked God to leave and now we are paying the price. I think he's right. Everything from abortion and deadbeat dads to the penal system is running amok. Filth is prevailing on television screens and on our computers. Rap music is detailing a perverse and promiscuous lifestyle that is being emulated by our youth. Drag queens are winning beauty contests and homosexuals are leading congregations. The amount of absolute sickness that is at our fingertips is enough to make a person's blood boil. A quick glance at a few of these problems will hopefully shed some light on our culture as a whole.

Part 2: Deadbeat Dads

In our culture we have many babies born into single parent homes. It appears to be most prevalent in the inner cities, but the numbers are rising in every race and walk of life. Whatever the percentage and whatever the skin color, it has a downward spiraling effect on society. If a young boy is raised without a father, then he will have little if any idea how to be one. Furthermore, we emulate the ones we respect the most, and for a young boy, that will generally be his father. If his father is out of the picture, then his mother will become the empress of his world. This generally leads to a disrespect of women and especially the mother of their own children, because nobody can compare to their own mother. Therefore, when a young boy has a father in the house that is respectful and dutiful in raising his family, then that particular child will have a far better chance of following in those same footsteps.

That is basic psychology, but it is lost on many of our social leaders. Bill Cosby has been a voice of reason in the black communities and he has been lambasted for his efforts. It's funny how the truth is considered evil these days. Regardless of your ethnic background or social status, you need to be responsible for your offspring. The matter gets even more hopeless when we realize that deadbeat dads generally are not God-fearing young men. I suppose it is possible to have a love for God and abandon your children at the same time, but I can guarantee you that it is as rare as Joan Rivers missing an appointment with her plastic surgeon. So what do we do to help rectify this problem? We could continue blaming society and the social environment, but that hasn't proven too effective thus far. Here's my idea.

First, we seek and identify who these guys are. We now have DNA testing that will help in the process. Then we educate them and the mother of their children on theology and morality. Personal responsibility is the key, but only half of the story, because if a man has no fear of God, then consequences lose their luster. If men can identify who gave them the ability to become personally responsible, then they will be more prone to acknowledge that the giver of their ability will someday hold them accountable. God has been left out of most equations when dealing with this problem, and maybe, just maybe, that is why the problem continues.

Secondly, after identifying these guys and re-educating them, we need to hold them financially responsible. If they cannot provide for their children, then we need to place them in work camps. They will be imprisoned in the fact that they will not be able to leave, but they will be treated well, fed well, and have decent living conditions. During their time at these work camps, they can learn valuable skills, doing the work that saves the taxpayers money. They can work the roads, help build bridges, whatever is needed, and the money earned will go directly to their abandoned families. Throwing these guys in jail isn't going to feed their children. Each evening, they will learn about God and morality, as there are countless volunteers who will help in this cause. We can have libraries and instructors to help these guys learn other skills as well to become productive members of society. When it is deemed that a deadbeat dad can provide for his children in the private sector and he is current on support payments, he will be released. Upon release, he will hopefully have a renewed idea about doing the right thing. When a deadbeat dad gets released from a typical jail, he has been a burden to the taxpayer and has only learned new ways to be more corrupt. I realize that there will be a fight as to which God will be discussed and the morality taught, but maybe we should teach about the God on which our country was founded and the morality contained therein—unless we plan on releasing these guys in Antarctica.

Part 3: Abortion

Whenever I encounter a theist who is pro-choice, I always give them this particular scenario to chew around in their obviously scattered brain. Imagine you are pro-choice and having a relaxing evening watching television, sipping on carrot juice, and scarfing down tofu because you care so much about the animals. Suddenly, your roof is torn open and God appears before you in all his glory. In reality, you would probably be vaporized by his glory, but hey, it's a scenario. You have never been surer of anything in your life: this is God and he has something to say and you can do nothing but listen and then respond in the manner instructed. In an authoritative voice, God says, "I am the Creator of all things. I give you your every breath. There is a heaven and there is a hell. In one minute, you will enter one or the other. I will ask you one question. Your answer will be either yes or no and it will determine your final destination. On the matter of abortion, do I, the God of the universe believe in a woman's right to choose?" To an atheist, the question is annoying at best, but to a person who claims to believe in God, it is gnawing at their very existence.

To the secularist, abortion is their sacred cow. It is legal and accepted by much of society, and because of the appalling nature of the act, it has become the greatest of victories for the progressive mindset. If people can accept the barbaric practice of abortion, then the sky's the limit. In order to change the frequency of this wicked practice, we need to solicit God and all the wisdom of those who know him. People find it easy to imply that a particular situation is not their business as long as they refrain from the practice. What are we, France? The most helpless among us are being snuffed out prior to taking their first breath and it's not our business? We have many powerful entities and politicians who are making it their personal business to defend this evil practice, and we sit around saying, "To each their own." Abortion has become a multi-billion-dollar business, and some people dedicate their entire life to insure that we continue this savagery. One legal decision does not make something right; we need to stand up and deliver. The Lord's Prayer doesn't say deliver *me* from evil—it says deliver *us* from evil. We are called upon to help our neighbors, and when our neighbors are in agreement that abortion is expectable behavior, then they need our help, and more importantly they need God. So here's an idea.

First we need to recognize that abortion is wrong and be willing to see it as such.

Secondly, we need to make all abortions public record. We need to place on display the women having abortions in newspapers and on television. To a secular progressive, having sex out of wedlock is considered inevitable and normal. The secular progressive also sees an abortion as the responsible action to be taken when a pregnancy results from our inevitable and normal deeds. Let's look at this situation a little further; words like *normal, inevitable,* and *responsible* are considered quality virtues in our language, and therefore adhering to these virtues should be deemed as good. We can then conclude that to a true believer in the progressive movement, any idea of shame should be negated for a woman who finds herself pregnant and waiting in line at the clinic. If there is no perceived shame in their freedom of choice, then they can see the free publicity as a moment of fame. Do I dare intend to display the actions of these poor women? Absolutely! I realize that this would be a safety issue for the (would-be) mothers and their families from the radical fringe and that precautions would be in order, but who is taking the necessary precautions to protect the unborn?

Also, we need to report accurately the numbers of abortions and the doctors and healthcare workers who perform these procedures. We should know their names and their affiliations and have complete disclosure of their funding. We should know the roots of organizations like Planned Parenthood and other state-funded institutions. Reading their brochure at the county fair would lead us to believe that these organizations are being led by June Cleaver. The truth behind these groups and their founders is disturbing at best and the people behind the curtain will make you shiver. We should be allowed to have present at every consultation a pro-life advocate as well as a Christian pastor to give alternative information to the mother.

Finally, we need to teach young mothers about morality and that it comes from God. The guilt that is felt by most women having abortions doesn't come from being irresponsible; it comes from an ultimate detachment from above.

Part 4: Rap Music and the Prison System

Chances are, you are not going to be the next Michael Jordan or Sean "Puff Daddy." Combs. If you live in the inner city, and if dealing drugs and gang banging seems to be the only alternative to the aforementioned careers, then you have a problem and your problem is becoming societies. Snoop Dogg makes millions upon millions glorifying the gang banger mentality and then retreats to his mansion that is far removed from the projects. The hip-hop mentality will lead the emulator to prison nine times out of ten, and sadly, the proprietors of this garbage couldn't care less. They are narcissistic in their every step, and though they might throw a little charity at the inner city from time to time, do they really care? The logical answer is no. Hiding behind the idea that they are merely reflecting the culture of the hood is really getting tiresome.

Would it kill these guys to sing a song or two about the possible hope of rising above the circumstances and making your way to greener pastures? How about mixing in a rhythm that isn't negative or angry and maybe a song that isn't degrading or full of vulgarity would be a nice change. The inner cities of our nation are on fire and these idiots are bombarding them with gasoline while making a profit for their misguided efforts. Their messages are clear: the police and white people are evil, your women and bling are your possessions, and the reason for your lot in life is everybody's fault but your own. White kids love this garbage as well, but many have an advantage, in that most white kids have a more structured support system complete with a father.

The inner cities are jam-packed with kids who in many cases have only brothers, uncles, and cousins to look up to as role models. Unfortunately, in many cases, their role models are poisoned by the hip-hop craze as well. The cycle of imprisonment is a vicious one, though glorified in this decaying culture. In some neighborhoods, imprisonment is considered a rite of passage to becoming a man and there is little shame exhibited by some of these thugs when they are jailed. Likewise, there seems to be little fear of imprisonment, and it has merely become a way of life for some. If you've been through the system a few times, then you lose the fear of what to expect, especially when inmates are allowed to hang out all day being unproductive.

If we change the prison system to twelve hours a day of hard labor, maybe the uncles and cousins would try a little harder to live a life outside of crime. Furthermore, they might encourage their younger family members to do the same. Once again, this could reduce the burden on the taxpayers, and be good for the human spirit of the inmate with the knowledge of accomplishment on a daily basis. Regardless of what changes are taken in the prison system, we should feel convicted to do something. There needs to be a fear of consequences in order for correction (which we could say is only common sense). I would then ask, "Just how common is good sense these days?"

Part 5: They Call It "Dope" for a Reason

Marijuana use truly is a gateway to other drug use, but marijuana alone is a downward spiraling nightmare in and of itself. According to the National Institute of Drug Abuse (NIDA), 40 percent of high school seniors have tried marijuana at least once, admittedly, and Lord only knows how many lie about it. The NIDA also reports that users of marijuana have a 60 percent greater chance of moving on to harsher drugs in the future. Any drug use is ridiculously stupid, but strangely, it is described as "recreational" in today's culture. In reality, becoming less intelligent should be recognized for what it is: a nightmare.

Putting aside the fact that smoking marijuana can lead to cancer, lung disorders, and a breakdown of the immune system, the mental disabilities alone should place a scare into every puff. The main active ingredient in marijuana is THC. THC binds to and activates specific receptors in the brain known as cannabinoid receptors that control memory, thought, concentration, time, depth, and coordinated movement.

Basically, you may lose track of the time when you forget to concentrate on the depth of the road ahead as you crash into a tree. After the crash, you may try to remember the thoughts that were rattling around in your brain prior to the crash, but the sight of the pine cones landing on your hood are far too humorous to allow for any reflecting on the incident. In other words, without exception, pot makes you stupid and that is why they call it dope.

I guess that I'll never understand why people will spend good money and risk criminal charges or possible imprisonment to become stupid. It has been well documented that long-term marijuana use can lead to personality disorders, depression, and social anxiety while the user becomes less and less able to recognize these derailments. I have several friends who started smoking marijuana in high school in the early eighties and never stopped. These particular friends have mostly lost their ability to engage in any meaningful conversations, as they have retreated into familiar dark havens where they watch a lot of cartoons and miss a lot of social events. Basically, it would appear to me that they stopped mentally maturing at the point that they began partaking in the substance and have remained there ever since.

Habitual marijuana use makes you a stupid social outcast, but an even greater atrocity is the bloodshed that occurs in the process of obtaining the green. According to an AP report listed in *USA Today,* it is estimated that the Mexican drug cartels are currently a 14 billion-dollar industry, and more than 60 percent of that blood money comes from marijuana use at 8.5 billion dollars annually. It is important to realize that these cartels reach into every corner of the United States. If you smoked a marijuana cigarette today, chances are extremely good that it placed money into the hands of these barbarians. Six thousand people were murdered last year alone in border towns in Northern Mexico that were directly related to the drug problem and this number doesn't take into account the numerous deaths that ensued on our side of the border. The murderous gangs that peddle this brain-reducing garbage are only the igniters of the problem; the countless lives that are ruined every day throughout our culture finalize the equation.

The American potheads are the real culprits. They are usually found wearing tie-dyed shirts and talking about government atrocities while they directly support the slaughter of entire families, including small, innocent children at the hands of their suppliers. If small children are dying every day so that you can fill your brain with chemicals that can only make you stupid, then maybe it's time to rethink (if you still have the ability) your actions.

Most marijuana smokers are shackled by their use in the same way as an alcoholic. If watching movies appears more entertaining while intoxicated, then they will avoid watching movies when their stash runs out. If they enjoy lighting up and playing ping pong, they will light up before every match and believe that they are playing at an extreme level. My high school water polo coach used to say sarcastically to a few bloodshot glaring eyes that if you are going to get high before a game, then you might as well get high before every game, because at least you'll think that you are playing at a high level. Pot heads are removed from the general public and usually remain in close proximity to other users because they use marijuana to enhance whatever activity that might amuse them. Being around straight-minded, sober persons will infringe upon their activities; the natural sense of paranoia that ensues from smoking pot in the first place makes the sober person appear threatening.

The Mexican government is currently moving to legalize marijuana and tax whatever portion possible. It would appear as if profiting off the vast drug problem is of their main concern while ignoring the war on drugs effort that is being waged by their neighbors to the north. I use the term "war on drugs" lightly because it has become a multi-billion-dollar industry in and of itself. If we couple the fines and legal fees of the captured with the allotted federal funding, this war is takes on a new theme. It is only through the cessation of drug use by the majority of users that the problem will ever form a sense of control. So how do we stop users from partaking in this senseless herb?

Obviously, most marijuana users are not God-fearing individuals. They may be god-loving individuals but their god is usually a rock, a mountain, a stream or a late-night chat room or television show. The god factor plays a role in every social ill that encompasses us today, but in the problem of drug use, it is most relevant. If every drug user came to realize that there is a God and that taking drugs will lead to an erosion of their ability to communicate with him, then the problem would lessen greatly. Beyond that, it would make sense to show images of the maimed and murdered bodies as a result of these cartels to young students starting in middle school and force them to acknowledge the user's responsibility. These images should be bouncing off every television screen in America at an appropriate time and on a nightly basis. As a society, we can place more pressure on users to quit with the devastating factors of their use clearly on everybody's mind.

Finally, we need to place on display video interaction of lifelong marijuana smokers for all to see. There are many pot heads among us who would love to participate in a documentary of this sort and probably wouldn't even notice the ridicule. Watching the fumbling, idiotic actions of some of these users, complete with that annoying "pot laughter." should be enough to scare most potential users straight.

Just a Thought #9

If whatever you are doing is wrong and you have little fear of the consequences, you are in the process of eroding your chances to correct that behavior. Getting caught should only be the first half of the equation; suffering the consequences completes the process. There is a problem when the suffering is left out, because through suffering, we learn. If a person has a fear of God, then they will quickly realize that what we suffer in this life will pale in comparison to eternal suffering. God gave us a conscience people: Use it!

Chapter 15

Holy Books and Philosophies

If your world view or philosophy doesn't answer the four questions of origin, destiny, morality and meaning, then your worldview or philosophy is completely bankrupt.

   Rick Booye

If you are a Christian, you are free to think that all these religions, even the queerest ones, contain at least some hint of the truth.

   C. S. Lewis

Part 1: Where to Begin

In this chapter, we are going to break down a few belief systems to their basic nuts and bolts. We are going to take a look at six different faiths, and I will do my best to point out the fallacies contained in each. I will admit that I am biased in my analysis, but my findings are based in logic and the historical record. If you don't believe in the historical record and using logic is not your thing, then this chapter will be of little help. If, on the other hand, you like using logic and you hold history with any level of esteem, then you might find this information useful. I do not intend to offend a follower of any faith, but I realize that I probably will, so this is for you:

"Sorry."

The first three faiths that we will look at are illusory faiths. This simply means that they believe, to differing degrees, that existence is just an illusion. They borrow from each other but not from the Bible. The remaining three faiths that we will examine base their origins directly from the Bible. Combined with the many denominations of Christianity and the Catholic religion, these six faiths make up approximately 85 percent of the world's population. If you throw in the remaining new and so called improved ideas to Eastern thought and atheism, then you have just about everybody in the canoe. The examination of these faiths will give us a better understanding of the overall worldview of all inhabitants on this planet.

If you were plopped onto this earth and had no idea as to where you came from, your first question would most likely be, "Where did I come from?" If you were granted the answer to that question, you would follow up your question with, "Where am I going?" If that question were answered, you might ask, "What is considered permissible behavior while I'm here?" And finally, "What is the reason for me being here?" People have been asking these questions since the dawn of man, and mankind has written many books explaining our answers to these questions. Some of these answers are merely personal ideologies that are easily dismissed as having little insight to the greater questions. They are filled with vague human emotions that have no real bearing on the actual questions themselves. If you examine the holy books of the world, you will see a pattern that is only interrupted when you compare them to the Bible. Man- made religion is actually very easy to discern. It only requires that you perceive them from a God's-eye view, because trying to make sense of man-made holy books from our personal view will leave you in a state of confusion.

Trying to see something from God's perspective requires the realization that we are flawed. And if we realize that we are flawed, then we must require intervention. And if we require intervention, then we need a being that is perfect to intervene. And if there is a perfect being who is willing to intervene, then he ought to have our attention. And if he has our attention, then we will soon begin to see how he views things. And if we can see how God views things, then we can (on a limited basis) have a God's-eye view. In other words, it only works for the true believers.

"As a Christian, I see many new things and I see old things in new ways."

Rick Booye

On the following pages, we will look at many religions and philosophies that inhabit our culture. After examining their main content and the core tenets of each, we will use logic and reason to determine their virtues and their flaws. Finally, we will compare each against the Christian perspective.

Part 2: Hinduism

Hinduism doesn't have a formal guide or doctrine. It does, however, hold several beliefs that need to be examined in order to have a better understanding of this philosophy. A quick look at the terminology will get us started

Brahman is ultimate reality.

Monism is at the core of Hindu thought. It is the idea that we are all related to ultimate reality and everything else. In other words, we are one.

Dharma regulates all the life forces that are *one* and regulates a continuous cycle known as reincarnation.

Karma is a law of cause and effect. Karma (unlike the Buddhist idea of reaping your rewards, either good or bad, in your next life) offers no guarantee until an undetermined point in time.

Maya is the idea that everything perceived is an illusion. Everything is a false reality, but to be taken seriously. If you see something horrific, it is just an illusion due to you through karma.

Samsara is the endless cycle of change. Everything is in the process of becoming something else.

Manu is the first man created from Brahman. Manu led to different classes of people.

Caste system is the classing of different people according to status. It is important to realize that to a Hindu, these classes have no significance. Since there are endless lives that lay ahead, life can be lived with a sense of contentment.

Moksha is a release of the cycle of reincarnation and the pains of life.

Now that we know the terminology of Hinduism, what does it all mean? What do they actually believe? Basically, the Hindu believes that all things are one and that Brahma is ultimate reality and produced the first man known as Manu. A Hindu's perceived reality is an illusion dictated by karma. If you do good deeds to a certain degree, then your illusions will be good to that equal degree. On the other hand, if you behave badly, then your illusions will be perceived badly. Dharma is in control of your illusions. There is a god or many gods, depending on which Hindu you ask, but they are not personal and have no control over your illusions. Only the law of Dharma can regulate the perception of your illusions. Hindus believe that all things are in a constant cycle of change and that cycle is called Samara. Hindus seek to end their personal cycle of reincarnation through Moksha, and it is left to each Hindu to find his own pathway. There are three ways to achieve Moksha, depending on which sect of Hindus you ask.

The first is a merit system known as Karma Marga. It entails that you do the correct rituals of your particular caste in all stages of your life. The second path is to embark yourself in yogic meditation to find your true self. This path can lead to Moksha in your current life. In the West, we are most familiar with the Bhatki Marga path, which became popular during visits from Hare Krishna in the twentieth century. This path requires a devotion to one of the many gods of the Hindu faith and bargaining with him. It is done in most cases with a guru as a guide.

There are vast difference between Christianity and Hinduism. Hindus believe that we are all one, including God, and that the physical realm is an illusion. Christians believe that we are separated from God through sin, but the physical realm is real and a reflection of God. Hindus believe that man is on equal footing with a tree or a porcupine. Christians see man as being created in God's image, and therefore the highest of life forms. Finally, Hindus believe in self-salvation through devotion, meditation, or bargaining. Christians believe in a divine salvation from God's grace through faith.

Hinduism has a hint of truth, but very little historical basis, and the philosophy can be quickly discarded by logic. To believe that physical realm doesn't exist is a giant leap of faith, and to believe that you can create a higher level of existence without intervention is a leap over the Grand Canyon with bad knees.

In the end, Hinduism leaves its followers with many unanswered questions. Human origin is vaguely answered by the teaching that Brahma or ultimate reality (which is said to have created the first man), but it never explains what ultimate reality is. Our destiny is only described as reaching a new level of existence departing from our cycle of numerous lives but there are little details of that new level. The meaning of life is to reach that new level on a personal journey, but the journey is merely an illusion. The morality in Hinduism is to do the right thing in whatever life has allotted you in the caste system, but it never reveals where right and wrong came from. Basically, Hinduism leaves the follower asking questions, and is therefore, at least in my mind, bankrupt.

Part 3: Buddhism

Unlike Hinduism, Buddhism has a founder and a historical basis. Although its founder, Siddhartha Gautama, based his foundation on Hinduism, he found a problem with suffering. His early attempts at meditation had little, if any, effect on his dilemma. After a several dreams of a world without suffering and death, he settled under a tree, entered a new level of enlightenment in three stages, and became Buddha.

The first two stages are entrenched in Hinduism. He first saw his previous lives pass before him, then he saw the cycle of reincarnation and the laws that govern it. The third stage, however, separates his philosophy from Hinduism. They are known as the four noble truths: the knowledge of suffering, the truth of suffering, the source of suffering, and the removal of suffering.

Buddha believed that all of life is *Dukkha,* which means that life is full of pain and suffering. He believed that people only have an illusion that things will get better, but were truly looking forward to a place of lesser pain. Since the life cycle is endless through reincarnation, then so too is pain. He believed that one must escape this cycle of pain and reach nirvana. Nirvana is a state of mind where permanent bliss is achieved and pain is absent. To reach this higher level, one must live outside of the illusion of ignorance. Buddhists believe that one must shatter the illusion of desire and ego and finally dispel the idea that we will placed in a permanent state of contentment or torment without reaching nirvana.

Buddha taught the way to nirvana in his "Eightfold Pathway."

1) Belief in the four noble truths.

2) Commitment to dispelling the human dilemma of suffering.

2) Carefully watching what we say to others.

4) Abstinence from intoxicants and treating all living creatures well.

5) Performing a job which does no harm to others.

6) Be in a good mood and having good thoughts.

7) Using your will to use all your energy in life.

8) Meditation.

When using the "Eightfold Pathway." it is said that it will dispel the pain caused by ignorance, release the ego, and allow one to find nirvana.

I wish there were more to it, but there really isn't. Though many books have been written since the days of Buddha, they merely expand on ways to meditate and to expedite the road to nirvana. I realize that the Buddhists of the world will have much more to say on the subject but they will be hard-pressed to escape the fundamental principles that make up the general philosophy.

The greatest difference between Christianity and Buddhism is man's origin. Buddhists believe in a naturalistic universe full of suffering. Christians believe that a personal God created the universe and man for his glory. Secondly, Buddhism focuses on one aspect of life—suffering and pain—where as Christianity focuses on all aspects of life. Finally, Buddhists believe that Buddha himself should be revered and honored as one of many gods who are not personal. Christians believe in one God who is personally involved. There are other stark differences as well, but you get the point.

Buddhism, like Hinduism, leaves its followers with many unanswered questions. It gives no explanation for the origin of a universe full of pain, just that it is full of pain and suffering. It has a destiny but gives little explanation of what it will be like when achieved. It only inquires as to one actual aspect of the meaning of life. As to the morality contained in Buddhism, while similar to Christianity in the sense of humility, it leaves out the bulk of the remaining aspects, including any idea of where morality came from in the first place.

In the end, I found Buddhism bankrupt as well. This would explain the constant packaging and repackaging of Eastern thought for our amusement throughout the ages. *The Secret* (that we discussed earlier) is the latest example, but there will be many to follow. Whenever you take sovereignty out of the hands of God and place it into your own hands, you are embarking on a journey east.

Part 4: Scientology

Scientology is a belief system developed from the writings of L. Ron Hubbard. Hubbard was a science fiction writer in the 1930s. In 1948, he wrote *Dianetics: The Modern Science of Mental Health*. The idea was to promote perfection in mental, emotional, and spiritual aspects of life. In 1952, Hubbard renamed his work *Scientology* and declared it a religion. Though it was declared a religion, it is non-theological. Basically, God is not mentioned in any Scientology rituals. The eradication of negative thoughts known as *engrams* is their only tenet. These engrams were said to be received in our embryos or from past lives. The Eastern influence is apparent, but Scientology offers a shortcut that makes it more appealing than going through the many distasteful lives during the reincarnation process. The idea is to find and overcome the original engram, thus allowing us to live without any encumbrances. Though it is a shortcut in time, it is much more expensive than its predecessors. It is not uncommon to spend hundreds of thousands of dollars to eradicate that original engram. Once it has been eradicated, a Scientologist will reach and cross what is known as the "Bridge to Total Freedom."

This is where Scientology gets a little weird. Okay, it gets unbelievably weird. This misery that needs to be cleared from each individual is said to have originated 75 million years ago when an evil warlord named Xenu sent billions of human souls to earth. These souls (which Hubbard called "Thetans") were plopped into volcanoes and then blown up with hydrogen bombs. These Thetans are everywhere and still exist today. They cling to all human bodies and infect them, and this is the primary cause of all misery. The good news is that for a boatload of money and countless hours of Scientology "auditing." you can get rid of these little buggers. This "auditing." can begin after you clean yourself with vitamins and steam. Once clean, you are considered "clear." and are then ready to proceed. In this auditing process, you sit adjacent from a Scientology "auditor." who assists you in your eradication of the Thetans. During this process, you are known as a "pre-clear." You are advised to relive unpleasant moments that are filed in your reactive mind. The auditor has a device called an E-meter which apparently can detect the engrams with electric pulse meters while gripped by the pre-clear. Through repeated confessions of the pre-clear, the engrams can no longer be allowed to cling to the Thetans. Many personal questions are asked with an emphasis on sexual morality. This is because Hubbard was a propionate of the teachings of Freud.

That is pretty much all there is to Scientology. It is a self-improvement philosophy that is clearly self- centered. Their origins are laughable, but there numbers are growing, especially among the rich and famous (which makes sense, because as we've learned, they think they're better than us and never has there been a religion or philosophy that clearly caters to an already inflated ego). Focusing on the here and now, Scientology offers little in regards to the hereafter. Therefore, answers of destiny are left to self-realization of one's own divinity. Morality and meaning are illusions and therefore not conveyed other than the expensive process of determining them as illusions.

Once again, the follower is left empty and bankrupt. It is interesting that in order to explain suffering and pain, Hinduism, Buddhism, and Scientology describe our existence as illusory. That puts up a giant red flag in my mind simply because it offers a quick, childlike answer to a tough question. When faced with a tough question about existence, stating that everything we perceive is an illusion erases all concern about actually answering said question and should, therefore, be disregarded.

Prior to moving on and to be fair, it should be noted that I am by no means an expert on the Eastern thought process and the depiction of said faiths noted above is a mere overview. I realize that there are many Buddhists and Hindus who deny the idea of an illusory existence and that these religious convictions have branched into many forms.

There are many followers of Eastern thought who can and will find my brief descriptions as vague and shallow, which to a certain degree is true. If I were to someday write a book about Buddhism or Hinduism, then maybe I'll leave the shallow end and venture further, but for now, it will remain my intention to shed light on the basic and core tenets contained in each.

The following belief systems differ from the prior in that they derive their faith directly from the original biblical scripture. These religions have founders, all of whom were entrenched in the biblical thought process prior to obscuring the original and creating a spin-off.

Part 5: Mormonism

Mormonism was founded in 1820 right here in America by Joseph Smith. At the age of fourteen, Smith claims to have been visited by Jesus and God. Three years later, he was visited again by certain angels in the form of previous humans: John the Baptist and three apostles. It was during these visits that Smith composed the Mormon Doctrine. According to Smith, he was chosen to restore the original doctrine of Jesus because it had been messed up through the years. Smith was a kook; a quick look into his formative years will reveal his overactive need to be noticed. Putting aside the gold tablets that contained his newfound information and the fact that only he was allowed to see them, we can dispel the authenticity by the fallacy of what they contained.

Smith claimed that the origin of the gold tablets that contained his newfound doctrine was traced back to 600 BC. That is interesting, because there are quotes in the doctrine that are taken directly from the New Testament, which as history tells us, began with Jesus at 1BC. Secondly, it is filled with scenarios of American life that didn't exist in 600 BC. Finally, Smith has made claim that he copied the words exactly as they appeared on the tablets; however, the language that was copied did not exist in 600 BC. The contents were translated in the King James Version of the Bible that didn't exist in the time of Jesus little yet 600 years before his birth.

The main tenets of the Mormon faith are contained in the Book of Mormon, as well as their doctrine and covenants (along with a splash or two from the Bible in order to sell the idea to the Christians at the time). Where Mormonism separates itself from historical Christianity is at Christianity's core. Mormons believe that we can obtain godhood and be equal to Jesus Christ. They also believe in a living prophet who can have new revelations that cancel the current doctrine. They are polytheists believing that the Father, Son, and Holy Ghost are three separate gods and finally, they believe that Smith himself should be exalted and worshipped as a prophet of God.

Beyond the basics, Mormons are forced the unenviable task of changing the pure nature of man as described in the Bible. If we are to become as God, then we must omit the fall of Adam, and the Mormons do this in a clever way. Eve was immortal and fell, but Adam was forced to choose between two separate commands: either don't eat from the tree and become mortal like Eve or fulfill the command to be fruitful and multiply. This, of course, explains the lower status of Mormon women in their faith.

Mormonism has approximately 15 million followers, most of whom reside in the western portion of the United States. Although it is a relatively new religion, it is extremely aggressive in its missionary work. It should be noted that Mormons make up a mere 5 percent of the world's population, and their religion has had little success beyond the original place of its founding. If this newfound revelation had any real steam based in historical fact, then it would infiltrate the growing numbers of Christians far beyond the western half of its country of origin.

In conclusion, Mormonism must be seen for what it is (a spin-off of the original), a perversion of the intent of the original, and finally, a giant leap of pride exalting a fabricator and his followers to divinity. Mormonism does have answers for some of the bigger questions, but they are too far-fetched to be taken seriously. (That is, unless you consider yourself worthy of being a god.)

Just a Thought #10

When I was a kid, wearing Levi's jeans helped make you one of the cool kids, and virtually everybody wore them. At some point during grade school, a few kids started showing up for school in Tough skins jeans. They were a laughable copy of the one and only original Levi's that we all knew and loved. Tough skins jeans had that obnoxious loopity-loop design on the back pockets and a zipper in front. The material seemed to be made from something NASA developed, because they were virtually indestructible. They cost less too and parents found them to be a great value. Unfortunately for the Tough skins Company, their jeans never really took off. Children, just like adults, will stick with the original until something better comes along and that usually isn't a diluted copy of what they already have. This might explain why there are few Mormons outside the territory where the Bible has already been taught.

Part 6: Jehovah's Witnesses

Founded in 1870 by a biblical teacher, Charles Taze Russell, Jehovah's Witnesses are another spin-off of the original scripture. Russell told his followers that Jesus had returned to earth in 1874 and would return again in 1914 to set up his new kingdom. It is interesting how impatient these guys are. Everything has either just happened or is about to happen in their world of delusions. It doesn't take much deduction to see that they were wrong, because the first time that Jesus made an appearance; he shook the world at its foundation. If he had made an appearance in the twentieth century, I kind of doubt we would have missed it. Maybe that explains that while they have had a sprinkling of success overseas, here in America, they have yet to reach 4 percent of the population as followers.

Jehovah's Witnesses are unlike the Mormons, in that they really have no doctrine. It is left to church leaders to decide what is to be believed and what is to be disregarded in regards to scripture. If you really want to learn about their faith, you need to find about five thousand different pamphlets that have been published over several years. These guys like to hand out flyers. In fact, the only person who really enjoys a Jehovah's Witness showing up at their door is the manager of a local print shop.

Through some simple research and a few clicks of the keypad, we can find some basic tenets of the faith.

First and foremost, they seem to have a fascination with the name Jehovah. It is very important to a Witness that they are the only ones who have this title of God correct and that all other names are blasphemy. Their reasons for this are as unclear, as they are unfounded.

Jesus is not God. He lived a perfect life, and his death was to redeem man, but he was merely human, and only his spirit was resurrected. It's funny to me that when something is hard for humans to swallow, they love to gut the theology and put it into human terms. This faith unfolds as believable in the eyes of a human and is therefore more plausible. It is unfortunate that they need to call the Apostles and Christ himself liars to do establish their faith, but hey, it's their ink.

Jehovah's Witnesses believe that the idea of the trinity is blasphemy. Any Christian who believes in one God (but in three persons) is considered a polytheist to a Jehovah's Witness. Once again, they find it hard for us to see or believe in something that is beyond our limited perception; therefore, it must be tweaked backwards into our earthly dimensions.

Rejection of celebrations is another of their restrictive tenets; Christmas, Easter, and birthdays are not celebrated in their faith. Their reasons for not celebrating are childlike; early Christians didn't celebrate Christmas, so why should we? Many of these celebrations stem from converted pagan holidays, so they are therefore to be deemed as evil and out of step. First off, in a sense, we are all converted pagans, so I say feel free to convert them all. Secondly, a Christian should always take advantage of every opportunity to bring attention to Jesus. A Jehovah's Witness is like a kid holding the book of rules and regulations while sneering at those who disobey it.

There are other crazy items that should be mentioned: no blood transfusions, Satan's general purpose, and the actual structure of the cross, but they keep the same theme. I liken the Jehovah's Witness to a modern-day political activist who forgot to do his research. They will be in a constant mode of "Gotcha!" pointing out the obvious and making a big deal out of nothing. So Jesus probably was not born on December 25? So what? It is a celebration that he *was* born. If you worship a calendar like Mayan enthusiasts, then the actual date of each event might matter, but to a Christian, it is a person of Christ who remains their primary focus. Unfortunately, for the Jehovah's Witness, they have ripped the heart out of the true meaning of the scriptures and therefore, they are only left with trivial arguments.

Once again, we are left with unanswered questions. Although a Jehovah's Witness can answer some of the bigger questions, he or she cannot explain their denial of the original scripture. It too must be conveyed as what it is: a perversion. It is bad enough to distort the revelation from God, but to sneer at you with only the words of a mere human to back them up, is beyond the pale. They are to be dismissed.

Just a Thought #11

When I was a kid, I loved playing Monopoly. I was the youngest of three brothers and we enjoyed the competition. My sister never really played much as she restricted herself to girly things and left the money-grabbing game to us boys. My brothers were always wheeling and dealing to put themselves in a better position and I, unwittingly (being the youngest) was at the core of their swindling strategies. They would tell me that four is better than two and I would trade my Park Place and Boardwalk for four railroads. It wouldn't be long before they were battling it out together and I was watching *The Three Stooges* in another room. Sometimes, the game would last for several days and my brothers would actually use an instamatic camera to photograph the board before heading to bed because they *loved and trusted* each other so much.

Just a Thought continued

There was one square on the board that always troubled young players: the 25 percent luxury tax square. The Monopoly man really let everybody down with that 25 percent tax. It would have been so much easier if they would have used 50 percent or 10 percent, as that 25 really threw the game into turmoil for us. It should be noticed that the game maker did change the square in later editions to a flat rate, an idea that is currently lost on the Internal Revenue Service. Eventually, as my brothers got older and actually read the rules, they went on to explain it to me. Then, as fate would have it, I tried to enforce the rule with a friend who was a tad younger than me and wasn't ready to give up 25 percent of his wealth. He and his sister, when landing on the tax square, always put a hundred dollars in the middle of the board for the lucky person who landed on free parking. This, by the way, is against the rules too but mostly accepted. Anyway, I used the rule book to plead my case, but eventually the matter was taken to his father, who would be both judge and jury, and as expected, his father sided with me. It's a good thing *that* didn't cause any problems. Obviously, it did. It not only ended the game, but it led to a seven-year-old claiming that the rule book was a misprint. He might have only learned the word *misprint* a week before, but he used it with impunity. Thirty-seven years later, we are still good friends, but I'm not sure if we ever played Monopoly again.

The point is this: I don't think that the Parker Brothers would have mass produced a board game and sent it around the world without being careful to read the rules and check for errors. Nothing is truer then when you are holding a Bible. It has always been and always will be the most reliable piece of historical literature that exists. If it is reliable, and it is, then who are we to make alterations to better suit us? The most scrutinized work of literature is the Bible and yet it remains the most mathematically reliable. The Hebrews followed by the early Christians went too far greater measures than the Parker Brothers ever dreamed of to insure the integrity of the Word.

Part 7: Islam

Islam makes up a sixth of the world's population and is growing at a rapid speed. Their birth rates are large and their doctrine is handed down from generation to generation with a complete absence of apathy.

The founder of the Islamic faith was their prophet Muhammad. Muhammad was illiterate; he grew up in Mecca, Saudi Arabia and was influenced by the Jews and Christians in the area who led him to a belief that there was only one God. Near the age of forty, Muhammad was meditating in a cave. There, he heard the voice of the Angel Gabriel, who told him that he was the final prophet of God. Muhammad had little success in converting others and was eventually forced to leave Mecca for Medina in AD 622. In Medina, he formed an army, and eight years later, he returned to Mecca and conquered it. Ten years later, Muhammad died. He continued to proclaim his belief in Allah and himself as the final prophet until the end.

Islam began to grow rapidly because of turmoil in surrounding areas. When weakened nations were most vulnerable, Islamic power would strike. They truly are a religion that was spread by the sword. Many converts were intrigued by the newfound simplicity of the faith, easy conversion, the elevation of peace, and brotherhood seemed to be pleasing to many. It is ironic that many of these tenets are lost on the modern Muslim. Muhammad himself forced his religion upon others, so it would then make sense that 1,500 years later, many are following in his footsteps.

The main tenet of Islamic faith is conversion. Simply stated, a convert is to profess that there is one God who is Allah, and Muhammad is his prophet. Muslims believe that their religion predates Judaism and Christianity, and although Jesus, Moses, and David are considered prophets, Muhammad has the last word. Though certain portions of the Bible are considered revelations from God, it is the revelation of Muhammad that supersedes them. This new revelation is contained in the Qur'an. The Qur'an is said to be a continuation of the Bible, but it contradicts the Bible in many ways. In the same manner of Mormonism, the Muslim is led to believe that the original scriptures are flawed through human corruption and that the new revelation is a correction revealed by God to Muhammad.

Islamic faith is practiced in what is known as the "Five Pillars."

#1: The Profession of Faith or "Shahada"
This is a profession of the core belief that Allah is God and that Muhammad is his prophet. The idea of the trinity is considered polytheism to a Muslim and is forbidden.

#2: Ritual Prayers
Five times a day, a Muslim is instructed to face Mecca and perform ritual prayer. Personal prayer is not done during these ritualistic prayers, but a Muslim is encouraged to be in a constant state of prayer that I suppose would be personal at some point.

#3: Payment of Alms for the Poor
Basically, it is an offering of your money to help the less fortunate. Though it has become a tax in certain regions of the Islamic world, there is no recorded amount. It is said to be levied to place all Muslims on equal footing before Allah.

#4: Fasting During Ramadan.
Ramadan is a month-long period that marks the period when Gabriel spoke to Muhammad. In the daylight hours during this month-long period, eating, drinking, smoking, and sexual relations are prohibited.

#5: Pilgrimage or Hajj
Every Muslim must make at least one trip to Mecca during his lifetime. It is done to promote brotherhood and equality within the Muslim community.

There are several different sects of Islamic thought, the largest being the Sunnis. (The word *Sunni* means "Way of the Prophet.") The Sunnis make up close to 90 percent of Islamic followers. A smaller group, known as the Shiites, makes up the bulk of the remaining Muslims. The Shiites place an emphasis on martyrdom because of Muhammad's cousin Shiat Ali, who was murdered defending the faith. The Shiites are considered the most radical of all sects of Islam, and they see most Sunnis as their enemy. They have a spiritual leader called an imam who has a divine right to lead all Islamic thought. It is obvious and plain to see why these two differing sects have a problem co-existing.

Islam differs in many ways from Christianity. It borrows from the original scriptures and then claims the original is flawed. Like Mormonism, it is limited to our understanding of the physical realm, and this automatically eliminates any idea of the Trinity. Though Jesus is a prophet in Islamic teaching, he is not considered the Son of God and was never crucified or resurrected. Islam goes as far as to deny the very essence of what God had previously revealed. If Jesus was a mere prophet, then his proclamations of being God were blasphemous. Muhammad never revealed how the message of the Bible became corrupt; he merely started a religion, helped spread it through violence, and died shortly thereafter. Jesus, on the other hand, filled the Old Testament prophecies to the letter and changed the very nature of those around him without lifting a finger to harm anyone.

In conclusion, we find similarities between these borrowed faiths. They seem to shy away from anything that cannot be easily understood while trapped in our limited dimensions. Simplicity is their most common thread while gutting the Bible to fit their radical changes from the original is their M.O. They feel the need to keep some remnants from the Bible in order to convert people who have a particular level of belief in the original. Starting a faith that is not founded in an existing religion is too high of a mountain to climb for the glory-seekers who seem increasingly impatient to see their new faith soar.

There really isn't anything new under the sun, and the line has been drawn between Eastern and Western thought. Either we subscribe to a belief that life is cyclical and illusory or we believe that there is a God who created the universe and life is what it appears to be.

Just a Thought #13

The most radical sect of Islamic faith is the Shiites. Similar to the book of Revelation, they believe in a tremendously violent end time. The Shiites believe that the twelfth imam will descend upon the earth in the last days after a period of wars and turmoil. This is eerily similar to the future prophecies pertaining to Jesus. The difference between this radical sect of Islam and Christianity regarding end times is, however, in stark contrast. The Shiites believe that it is their duty to cause the wars in the end times to summon the coming of the imam, while Christians are taught to love our enemies as ourselves and leave the vengeance to the Lord. There are a billion Muslims alive today, and it has been estimated that 10 percent are of the radical nature. That means that there are 100 million Muslims who feel that jihad is a duty and ushering in the end times is a worthy cause. It truly amazes me that there people in our society who feel that Christianity is an equal threat to our way of life as radical Islam is.

Chapter 16

The Assault on Faith

Part 1: Losing My Religion

Most Americans claim to be Christians. There are several denominations of Christianity, but the large majority of the population professes to be affiliated with one or another. My previous study did nothing to obscure these numbers. Amazingly, if it is true that approximately 80 percent of our population is Christian, then why would Christianity be the most scrutinized faith? I was under the impression that the majorities made the rules and were the oppressors. The problem is easily understood when we realize that the minority is the louder voice. The minority controls the media, the entertainment industry, and the learning institutions. Portions of the remaining majority are easily misinformed by these venues and are led like sheep to the slaughter, unwittingly at that. It is true that most informed Christians are conservative, but there is that remaining portion who can be brainwashed into believing just about anything—and these unsuspecting people are whom the attack is directly aimed at. The secularists are currently raging their attack in every aspect of American life and the Christian faith is their main focus.

A few years back, a commercial ran for one of the Yellow Pages advertisers. I can't remember which one, but I will always remember the ad. It featured a guy named Ed (we're calling him Ed because I can't remember his name) who had a rug store called Ed's Rug. He had only one rug in his store and was afraid to advertise in the Yellow Pages because somebody might actually buy his rug and then there would no longer be Ed's Rug. I found this ad to be hysterical. I also found it to be a great analogy for describing the difference between the secularist progressive thought that is mostly inhabited by anti-Christian ideology and the traditional thought process. If the rug were to be sold, then there would be no need for Ed—and if the secularists actually solved a problem, then the basic need for the secularists would erode as well.

The secularists like the problem, but they avoid the rational answers that might actually solve them. Why? To put it simply, they want to feel needed, just like Ed. To take it to the next level, they don't believe that you can solve the problem on your own, and that you require their keen intellect. A secularist, if he is a true believer in the ideology, has the notion that to make things fair, we must treat everyone differently. They scream about a level playing field, but insist on handicapping the players according to their abilities. A conservative or a traditionalist also likes a level playing field, but realizes that people are different, and that unless you treat them differently and insist upon a handicapping system, they will fall at different levels. This is not a mystery, as people have different levels of abilities and will need to find their own unique talent.

Before we expand too deeply into the reasons that Christians are at the forefront of this assault, I want to make it clear that the difference between a traditional conservative and a progressive liberal is not brain surgery. It can be easily understood and rationalized. The differing viewpoints will be continually argued and discussed by people who make it their life's work, but the actual opposition remains a simple equation. The ideologies of both can be displayed quickly in two analogies that I've come up with over the years to explain to the vast differences in simple terms. Throughout the years, I have met so many people who are under the impression that conservative Republicans are only for the rich and that liberal Democrats are for the working man. Not only is that a fallacy, but the opposite is true. These two scenarios might shed some light on the subject.

Part 2: The Easter Egg Scenario

Imagine there are two young mothers. One is a traditional conservative and the other a secular progressive. (Bear in mind that when liberals find their title to show any level of disdain, they quickly change their title). A progressive is still a liberal, but by a different name. Anyway, these two young mothers share one thing in common: they both have twin sons about five years of age. It is Easter Sunday and they head out to the community park where a large Easter egg hunt is about to commence. Both moms ready their kids with decorated baskets and make sure that their little tennis shoes are snugly tied to their feet. When the hunt begins with a loud whistle, the moms realize that they have something else in common: each has one boy who is adventurous and excited about the hunt and is collecting many eggs, and each has another boy who is crying, complaining, staying close to mom, and collecting only a few eggs.

This, in and of itself, is not a real problem, because any kid can have a bad day. The lesson that is learned from Mom, however, can be devastating. When the hunt ends, each mom has a direct chance to teach a life lesson to her boys. The secularist progressive mom tells her little achiever that it is only fair that we divide the eggs into equal portions so that our little complainer here gets his fair share. The traditional conservative mom will simply say to her little complainer that the eggs were out there and you could have had more, but you chose to complain and cry instead of finding them.

The lesson learned for the boys of the secular progressive mom is this: "Life will give you your fair share regardless of your actions. If you are ambitious, you will be punished, and if you are lethargic, you will be rewarded." The traditional conservative mom will convey the lesson that the park is open to all but you will need to be ambitious to receive your awards. Which lesson makes more sense?

The second analogy is more to the point of why the secularist progressive who has gained power will alter much more than playing field to retain power.

Part 3: The Pit

Imagine yourself in a pit. There appears to be no way out. It is advantageous for you to be in that pit for the secular progressive, because if he can point you out to voters decade after decade and instill the idea that they are the ones who really care about you being in the pit, they will then use this false sense of caring to secure the votes needed to remain in power. To show how much they care, they will walk by the pit from time to time to say hello and reach down to shake your hands. They will have their pawns(also known as bureaucrats) make sure that somebody throws you a can of beans from time to time and that you have plenty of water. They are selling you to the public and they need you alive with outstretched arms. Your condition will continue to be sold for as long as the American public continues to buy it. To me, Spam tastes and looks like cat food (yes it's true, I have older brothers and I have eaten cat food) but it is, amazingly, still being sold. Therefore, why not believe a clever lie that has the backing of the guy with the biggest bullhorn? It's like the moral of the kid who cries wolf—only in this case, the people never figure out that he's lying. If a traditional conservative sees you in the pit, he'll get you a ladder and be lambasted for not walking down the ladder and carrying you out on his shoulders.

The traditional conservative believes that a rising tide raises all ships. The secular progressive doesn't want all the ships to rise, because they would need to close their rug store and would no longer be needed. More than anything, they would lose their power.

To summarize the stark differences between the opposing world views, it can be said that the progressive has little or no faith in the ability of the downtrodden to rise up and render themselves useful, where as the conservative deeply believes in the human spirit of each individual and their ability to render themselves useful. The secularist needs the problem to exist to advance their cause, whereas the traditionalist needs to eradicate the problem to advance theirs.

So what does all this have to do with God? It's really quite simple: if a secular progressive is to retain the power, they need to bombard and devalue American tradition. They need ammunition, and social problems are their ammunition. There is no greater American tradition than Christianity, and the secular progressive sees Christianity as the final bridge that needs to be destroyed to achieve ultimate power. They scream about change, but few really understand the actual change they desire. They are elitists in their very nature, and they see Christians as stupid, ill-informed people who are standing in the way of progress. They will demean Christians at every turn, but will do it in a subliminal way because they are currently still in a situation where they need the Christian vote. A day will come when they no longer need our votes, and that is truly frightening.

It has been written that they will eventually prevail and all hell will break out, but that doesn't mean that it needs to happen on our watch. Are we going to be the generation that lets our traditional values escape us? Christianity is what holds our society together, whether we like it or not, and when it is devalued to a point of no return, then we will be ruled by people who simply feel that they know what is best for all of us. Basically, our ideas of freedom are at stake. The secular progressive proprietors of this war are well financed and organized, and they will never stop fighting. Maybe it's time to take the fight to them. They may possess the majority of microphones, but we still have the home-field advantage, because the last time I checked, this is still God's green earth. They have money, power, and Sean Penn, but we have history on our side and God hitting cleanup. I like our chances, but we need to move away from apathy and quickly right the ship. We need to entrench ourselves in history while it is still available to discern, and we need to step back to the values and traditions that made this the greatest nation on earth. More than anything else, we need to acknowledge God in all his glory and the tremendous blessings that he has bestowed upon us.

The war that is currently being raged over ideology is nothing new. If any political group is successful in a power grab, then they will become dangerous as it has happened throughout history, and the results are always the same. People in power become corrupt through pride and eventually, they write the rule book and oppress those who do not follow it to the letter. If the true believers in the secular progressive movement had their way, they would create a state religion, and this new religion would be used as a propaganda machine. Of course to anyone who reads history this is nothing new as it has happened throughout history in all oppressing civilizations. The scary part is that in the new revisionary history that is being taught we are the world's oppressors and Fidel and Hugo are seen as humanitarians.

Furthermore, this new State religion might make a mention or two about a universal force of goodness, but mostly it would prop up the greatness of the state and the duties of all under its rule. It would allow all faiths to worship, but never to a certain god that is exalted over another. Divinity would be regulated into a universal god that is non authoritative and weak. True believers of the Christian faith will avoid these gatherings and be forced to worship in hiding. The state will seek out these followers of the Christian faith and persecute them as traitors. Since Christians are in the majority, they will be the ones sought most. Hindus and Buddhists will pose little threat to the state and will be mostly left alone. Make no mistake: This scenario is coming to a town near you; it's just a matter of time. I think that it is prudent however, to hold back the tide as long as possible. I can't speak for everyone, but I like the traditional America complete with Sunday school and I want my son to experience it as well.

Here are a couple of revised sayings that show our changing mindset.

"A rising tide raises all ships."

Replaced by:

"A rising tide swallows the smaller ships and we need to spend trillions of dollars on life preservers."

Or:

"Give a man a fish and he'll eat for a day; teach a man to fish and he'll eat for a lifetime."

Replaced by:

"Give a man a fish and he'll eat for a day; teach a man to fish and he'll certainly exceed his limit, trash the environment, and become a greedy Republican."

You can call me an alarmist, but history says otherwise. Virtually all civilizations start out the same way with two prominent features: traditionalism and conservatism. They thrive until their traditions erode, and then they become corrupt and perverse through the power of a few. In the end, they crumble from within through the apathy of the majority. It happened to the Greeks and the Romans; it happened to Germany and the Soviet Union, and is currently on display throughout the third world. Secular progressive thought has spread like wildfire throughout modern-day Europe. Today, they live in a nanny state where personal morality is never to be judged. America is on that road as well, but we can still retain our traditions for a while. Knowing the end result is never a reason to be lethargic. It is in our nature to destroy all that is good, but in the same vein, it would be ridiculous to never do anything good for your health simply because you know that in the end you will die.

The chains that once linked us together as a nation have been severed. If we look back into our genealogy, we will find that most of our ancestors were deeply devout believers in one God. In most cases, their held belief was in the God of the Bible. Our nation defied all odds and became the greatest nation that ever existed, and in record time. Many can and will argue that our beginnings as a nation are blemished with atrocities, and that is true, but it is also true of all other nations. People are flawed and make mistakes, and some of those mistakes are diabolical. It is hard, however, to argue with the blessing bestowed upon us as a nation.

The problem is that so many Americans have never realized that our founding truly was a blessing. They are mainly focusing on the evil that has been perpetrated through man, while forgetting the good fortune that God has permitted us. Taking it a step further, the secular progressive is blaming God for our own misdeeds. Here's a news flash; God didn't shoot the Indians and God didn't scalp the white man. God blessed us to become a beacon of hope throughout the world and forsaking him at this dangerous point in history will result in dire consequences.

You will be told over and over again in the coming years that Christianity is the wedge that keeps us separated as a nation. Don't believe it. Christianity is the main ingredient that helped form this nation and the only ingredient required to restore it.

"America, America, God shed his grace on thee, and crowned thy good with brotherhood from sea to shining sea."

Katharine Lee Bates 1895

Part 4: Jesus Camp

I recently went through the painful event of viewing *Jesus Camp* because I had heard from so many people that they believe the film portrays modern Christianity. Before I ridicule the inaccuracy of that idea, we need to do some math. Though numbers vary, approximately 70 million Americans claim to be evangelical Christians, but in reality, the actual number is around 50 million. Now it's time to do some division to find the number of persons who adhere to the efforts of the Jesus Camp attendees. The film sheds light on one denomination of Christianity (the Pentecostals). The Pentecostals make up approximately 25 percent of evangelical Christians in the United States, which brings the number down to about 12.5 million. Okay, that is still a large number, but when we consider that only one person in ten of the Pentecostal Church believes that this film is an accurate portrayal of their core beliefs and traditions, the number shrinks considerably. There are 300 million Americans and one-third of 1 percent are radical Pentecostals who behave in the manner of the subjects in this film.

This perspective is lost on the two gals responsible for this film. Rachel Grady and Heidi Ewing had an agenda while filming this documentary and it is apparent by the absence of perspective achieved in the numbers listed above. They didn't do anything wrong; they just gave a group of kooks enough rope to hang themselves and kept the cameras rolling. In post-release interviews, they openly admitted that this movement is a subculture of Christianity, but in the same breath, they advised listeners that there are over 100 million Evangelicals. Cleverly avoiding true numbers will lead people to believe that there are 100 million crazy militant Christians out there trying to take over Washington, DC while speaking in tongues.

The film focuses on a radical pastor named Becky Fischer and a handful of children who attend her "Kids on Fire" summer camp in Devil's Lake, North Dakota. Fischer forgoes the idea of nurturing children into an understanding of scripture, and instead has them rolling around on the floor, riddled with guilt, crying, and speaking in tongues. Some of these children are no older than six, and it is quite apparent that they have little understanding of what is happening at the event other than the idea that pain and death are awaiting them if they don't get with the program. Eventually, Fischer has the children enacting ritualistic war dances with painted faces, while others fawn over a cardboard cutout of George W. Bush. The way these kids are used as political footballs is disturbing, to say the least. Toward the end of the film, the kids are found at the nation's capital, chanting some form of gibberish prior to taping their mouths shut with the word "Life" written boldly for all to see. In the end, what the film portrays is this: a few radical, charismatic, fundamental Christians who are very misguided themselves brainwashing the weakest among them (children) to behave as they do, while never offering a reason why.

Children can be led to believe just about anything in their formative years. These same kids could be equally as enthusiastic about witchcraft if their parents and spiritual leaders had led them down a darker path. Teaching our children about God is a good thing, but realizing that they are limited in their understanding and unable to relay a cognitive account for their belief must be recognized. Children reveal God's love by being who they are, not by acting out in the way that a particular radical sees fit. Just as an infant needs his mother's milk for nourishment, a child needs the milk of Christianity to develop his faith. The meat of Christianity is left to ears that can discern those ideas and grow in their faith.

Here is the message that the vast majority of small children learn at most Christian churches in America today:

"Jesus loves the little children, all the children of the world. Red and yellow, black and white, all are precious in his sight, Jesus loves the little children of the world."

That is a far cry from having kids rolling around on the floor, crying, and speaking in tongues. The problem with this film is that it is clearly used as propaganda against Christians. In an attempt to portray Christianity as a radical religion, these two moviemakers have forgone the truth contained in perspective and replaced it with their agenda of labeling Christians as lunatics. Obviously, they have a distain for the Christian faith and that supersedes their need for honesty. This is what liberal filmmakers do: they find something distasteful, exploit the most radical few contained therein, and display it as the norm.

Jesus Camp was a huge success; it has been seen by millions around the world and was even nominated for an Academy Award by other liberals. To your everyday, devout Christian (like myself), it is seen for what it is: an isolated situation where we find a group of misguided people who are abusing their rights as parents and leaders. To the non-believing secularist, it is seen as the typical church model and should be feared and denounced. The latter is the message that Grady and Ewing are trying to invoke, and it becomes apparent when we read the review that is used as a tag line on the back of the DVD box.

"A message that secular liberals and born again Christians have to listen to with open ears."

Evan Fisk, GO magazine

Look out! Here they come; they lurk in every church, on every corner, and they seem to be growing in numbers. Help us, Miss Grady! Help us, Miss Ewing! Somebody stop the madness!

Give me a break!

Just a Thought #12

Americans are not inherently any better than any other group of people. We are simply more blessed. To all of you true-blue nationalists who have forgotten that our way of life is a blessing, it's time to wake up and be a little more inquisitive as to why your grandfather still teaches Sunday school.

Chapter 17

Christianity in Layman's Terms

This is the chapter where we take a closer look at Christianity. We have had a glimpse into various faiths and discussed their main tenets, but now it is time to delve into the main faith held among Americans. It is here that I will describe in greater detail what I believe and why I believe it. Up until now, this book has been devoid of any biblical verses to back my findings, but rest assured, they are coming. I also have refrained from using the term *Lord,* because it seems to push people away from continuing their search. *Lord* implies obedience, and many among us have a real problem with good behavior and following rules. In this chapter, I will use the term *Lord,* because this is where I will profess my personal world view and why I believe Jesus is my personal Lord and Savior. I will break this chapter down into several sections that will explain different aspects of the Christian faith in easy-to-understand terminology. I will do my best to avoid being considered as an expert, because I am not. I do have a firm grip on the basics, and that is what I will try to convey. If this chapter strikes a curiosity in you, then I highly recommend that you seek out a local pastor who can help you in your search and who will pray with you in the hope that you will find what it is you're looking for.

"*I believe in Christianity as I believe that sun has risen. Not only because I see it, but because by it, I see everything else.*"

C. S. Lewis

"*In the beginning, God created the heavens and the earth.*"

Genesis 1:1

Part 1: The Basics

The Bible is a wonderland of information. A person could spend several lifetimes studying it and would still learn something new every day. Amazingly, the overall theme is relatively simple, as the whole story can be summarized into a short paragraph. This is by no means a reason to avoid reading; studying and learning from these divine words, it is merely to put an overview on the book itself. I have been asked on more than one occasion to quickly assess the overall story of the Bible. My answer is something like this.

God created the heavens and the earth. During this creation period, he created man in his image. He gave man free will and man chose unwisely and became an enemy to God, but God continued to love his enemy. At first, God spoke directly to man, but man continued to turn away from God, so God then destroyed the earth and started over with Noah. Still, men continued where they left off and turned away from God. Amazingly, God continued to love his enemy. God then revealed himself to a certain group of people (the Hebrews), but even they continued to turn away from God. Through nothing short of amazing grace, God continued to love his enemy. God then emptied himself into human form and became obedient to the point of death, to pave a way for our sins to be forgiven and to allow those who believe and have faith in him to be awarded his saving grace. His overall plan is to build his kingdom of the faithful and he administers his plan perfectly because he loves us. End of story.

Grace through faith is the answer to eternal life for the Christian, as it is impossible to build a stairway to heaven. God doesn't instill in us the ability to earn heaven, and we all fall short. He does offer us a way to heaven, and that is the good news (or gospel), but it can only be achieved through his eternal grace.

Part 2: The Scriptures

The Bible is divided into two testaments: the Old Testament (that is revealed before the time of Jesus) and the New Testament (that is revealed during the time of Jesus and shortly thereafter).

The Old Testament (also known as the Hebrew Bible), contains the books of Moses, which are also known as the Torah (or Pentateuch, which are the first five books of the Bible). These books contain an account of creation, the fall of man, and the exodus of God's people from Egypt. The next twelve books are called the historical books, and they contain the account of God's people from the entry into the Promised Land to their return to exile. The historical books are followed by the five wisdom books. These books concern themselves with the meaning of daily life; love, desire, pain, and suffering are described in these books. Many of these books are written as poems and songs of worship. The remaining seventeen books are called the books of the prophets. These books are divided into two forms of prophetic work. The former prophets are in narrative form and the latter prophets. The main focus of a prophet is to communicate the will of God, either past or future.

The New Testament is broken into three segments. The first segment is known as the Gospel of Jesus Christ. It contains four separate accounts of the life, ministry, death, and resurrection of Jesus. The gospel is comprised of the books of Matthew, Mark, Luke, and John. The next segment has only one book, Acts. It can be set aside from the following books only because it is not a letter. The book of Acts is the account of the Day of Pentecost (when the Holy Spirit was freely given as a gift into the hearts of the disciples). It also has an account of the beginnings of the Church, with Peter being the main focus, followed by Paul in later chapters. Finally, the last twenty-two books of the New Testament are called the epistles (or letters). These books are letters to early Christians in different geographical surrounding areas, and are mostly written by the Apostle Paul. The letters are named, in the most part, for the recipients of each letter, and they were written to help early Christians with their development in their newfound faith—and it does the same for us as well.

Now that we have examined the basic story of the Bible and we have seen a quick layout of its contents, it's time to examine it a little deeper. I've stated it before but nowhere is it more important than here. I am a layman in the arena of theology. C. S. Lewis called himself a layman on these biblical topics and he probably forgot more about Christianity than I will ever know. The very intent in writing this book is to encourage a state of curiosity that will hopefully develop into something special over time.

Part 3: The Core

This segment will be broken down into seven different sections. In each section, I moderately detail what I have found to be true. I will display some of the most common arguments against my beliefs and will submit other theological works in support of my beliefs. The seven sections are:

A) The Bible and Its Reliability
B) Faith and How to Obtain It
C) Grace, the Powerful Gift
D) Origins of Our Existence
E) Morality of Man
F) Meaning of Life
G) Heaven

I have touched on many of these subjects throughout the book, but now we are going to see where these ideas of mine stemmed from in the first place. In other words, I didn't make this stuff up; I read it, and God's will enabled me to understand it.

A) The Bible and Its Reliability

Cleland B. McAfee once asserted that you could literally place all the essential parts of the Bible back together from quotations from literature that is currently on the shelves of any public library.

Heaven and earth will pass away, but my words will by no means pass away.

Mark: 13:31

The Bible is the ultimate bestseller. The number of copies in circulation: in one form or another reaches into the billions. The book has faced many hardships. Throughout the ages, it has been banned, burned, and scrutinized more than any other work of literature. The Bible was written over a 1,500-year period by more than forty authors from every walk of life. It was written in three languages, on three continents, during times of joy and turmoil. The book contains all aspects of life—love, poetry, song, law, memoirs, prophecies, and parables. It truly is an amazing book, and holding a Bible in your hands should be awe-inspiring, even if you are not inclined to believe in the contents. The Bible has many characters but only one main character, God.

The Old Testament displays the law of God, the preparation for his coming, poetic songs that are meant for worship towards God, and the expectation of his next arrival.

The New Testament displays a record of Christ, the interpretation of Christ through the epistles, and the forming of the future kingdom in revelations.

Reading through 1,500 years of history and revelation would be a tiresome task if we were encumbered by the idea that the words were not a reliable translation of the original. So how reliable is the Bible?

To put it plainly and simply, it is the most reliable work of literature ever written and nothing even comes close. During the 1,500 years that the Bible was being created, it was copied by hand over and over again by Hebrews who made it their life's work to do so. During this long period, papyrus was used as a writing material. The material had a short lifespan, and the original scriptures were copied, reviewed, and recopied again at a constant rate. This was considered the most important job that a Hebrew could have. Every letter, syllable, and verse was to be perfect before it was passed on to be recopied. The scriptures were often back checked against copies that had been written years before to confirm accuracy. Nowhere else have we found such time invested in preserving a work of literature. Early Christians followed in their Jewish ancestors' footsteps by copying every letter with precise accuracy.

Manuscript is another word for a hand-copied version of the original. The oldest manuscript of the entire Old Testament is dated around AD 800, but the Dead Sea Scrolls are dated during the time of Jesus. When we compare these two manuscripts, we find 95.5 percent accuracy, with minor discrepancies. The New Testament has an even greater reliability record. We have found many manuscripts dating from AD 125 to 250 that have a 99.5 percent accuracy level when compared to any Bible printed today, and the discrepancies are mostly spelling errors or word order.

Skeptics have tried to denounce the reliability of the Bible using other writings, but their attempts have failed every time. The Bible is 2,000 to 3,500 years old and its reliability far exceeds that of William Shakespeare, whose work dates back four centuries—and he lived during the age of the printing press.

The Bible is divinely inspired and can be counted on for an accurate account of history and revelation.

B) Faith and How to Obtain It

Traditional Faith

"So that your faith might not rest on man's wisdom, but on God's power."

1 Corinthians 2:5

Today's Faith

"Faith has not always been as suspect a category as it has now come to be. Both the Hebrews and the Greeks had an understanding of faith. True, there were some differences, but still faith had legitimacy. Today, if faith is admitted at all, it is seen as the faith to have faith. It is packaged as a private matter and banned from intellectual credence.."

Ravi Zacharias

Faith is confidence. I have faith that my wife will continue to love me, and I am confident that she will do so. I have faith that the sun will rise tomorrow; while confident, I have no assurance. More than anything else, I have faith in the person of Jesus Christ. Regardless of how his will affects my personal life, I will remain faithful because of who he is. My faith is based in the knowledge of Jesus being who he claimed to be and I will remain confident that he will fulfill his promise to me for being faithful.

My faith grows stronger every day, but if the reverse were true, then I would need to re-assess my faith. I do have days were my faith is tested, but it only makes me grow stronger. Sometimes, I test my faith by trying to imagine myself not believing. Basically, I play devil's advocate with myself. I never get too far, simply because I have yet to find any other logical explanation for my existence, and my heart leads me back to Jesus. When a time comes in a person's life that he realizes that the Lord has revealed himself in word and in the creation, he tends to listen more intently and look a little closer.

The ability to obtain faith is a gift, as is everything in life—including your next breath. God gives us many reasons to have faith in him; he gave us eyes to see his beautifully created world, he gave us ears to hear his revealed words, and minds to understand them. He gave us a conscience to know right from wrong. He gave us love to settle our hearts and prepare us for his ultimate love. He performed miracles and rose from the dead and he has proven himself worthy of our faith, love, and devotion.

True Christian faith stems from "throwing up the sponge," as C. S. Lewis puts it in *Mere Christianity*. It is to say that when we as humans reach the point of realization that we cannot completely control our temptations, alone without intervention, it is then that we must surrender to God to steer our lives. If we surrender our imagined sovereignty to the rightful owner, we will have begun our venture down the path to meaningful faith.

Attempting to actually move from a feeling of belief to a conviction of faith requires humility; therefore, seeing yourself for the hopeless sinner you are is the key. Without this instrumental event happening in your life, true faith cannot be obtained.

"Who among you is wise and understanding? Let him demonstrate it by his good way of life, by actions done in humility that grows out of wisdom."

James 3:13

A few years back, I was helping coach my stepson's Little League team. It was an instructional league comprised of seven- and eight-year-olds, and the games were long and hopelessly boring to watch. Children at that age are easily distracted, to say the least. On a particular game day, Kyle had an accident at school; he had apparently fallen off the monkey bars and landed on his lower back. I picked him up early that day because he claimed to be in too much pain to remain at school, but as the afternoon wore on, he began to feel better. He even decided that he could play in the game later that day. Since I was the assistant coach, Kyle being able to play was a good thing. If I had to endure the maddening boredom, then it would make sense that he be there as well.

When we arrived at the field, Kyle was running and jumping, with no sign of pain. A crazy thing happened on his first at-bat that led to a much-needed life lesson: Kyle struck out. He slowly walked from the batter's box with his head down, and when the manager told him to hustle, Kyle wasn't in the mood. When questioned, he claimed that his lack of hustle was because of his injury earlier in the day. I gently informed him that if he couldn't hustle because his back hurt too much, he would need to sit out the remainder of the game. It was an extremely hot day, and that sounded good to Kyle and he quickly agreed. The following inning, as I was making my rounds through the infield, making sure that the kids weren't writing their names in the dirt with their cleats, I glanced over and saw Kyle running in circles behind the dugout. As I watched him at play, he performed some amazing actions for a kid with lower back pain. He hung from the chain-link fence a couple of times, kicked a soccer ball, and actually performed a few somersaults. Obviously, the pain was exaggerated.

On the way home, the interrogation began, and he immediately folded under the pressure. He admitted that he was hot, and that after striking out, he just didn't want to play anymore. Obviously, that didn't sit well with me. Later that night, I composed a simple letter that Kyle was to memorize and say to his team regardless of whether he wanted to continue playing or not. Basically, it read: "During the last game, I lied about my back hurting so that I could get out of the heat. I was also angry that I had struck out. I let the team down, but it will never happen again." Kyle had tears welling up in his eyes as he said those words to his teammates, but when he finished, an interesting thing happened. The manager tousled his hair and said, "Good job, Kyle." Kyle had removed a heavy boulder from his chest, and his tears were replaced with a shine and a smile.

Some people never learn those valuable lessons of humility. Most of us who do eventually learn to forget them as we grow older. Humility toward an invisible God is a hard pill to swallow for many, but it the only pill that will cure our illness and allow our faith to flourish.

C) Grace, the Powerful Gift

"For the law was given through Moses; Grace and truth came through Jesus Christ."

John 1:17

"For all have sinned, and fall short of the glory of God, and are justified freely by his grace through the redemption that came by Christ Jesus."

Romans 3:23–24

Grace is the free gift of salvation and it is unearned and not deserved. In the Old Testament, God showed mercy on his chosen people not because they deserved it, but because he loved them. If we have true faith in the risen Lord Jesus Christ, then we will be freely awarded his grace.

The term *grace* is defined first as a divine intervention for sanctification that is unmerited. Many people think of grace as being charming and charismatic (and that is true), but many words have multiple meanings, and we need to focus on the first definition.

God gives a certain level of grace to non-believers so they might find truth. God gives absolute grace to believers so that they will experience true freedom to act according to his purpose. With a complete absence of grace, the world would be in a constant state of hell. God's grace—while being the vessel in which we find eternal life—also acts as a buffer zone to allow the human race a period of time to seek the Kingdom.

Grace must be desired and sought. Through humility and faith, it can be obtained, but never based on our good deeds. A merit-based heaven is a misconception that many never fully understand. Even if you build a stairway to heaven, the gates will not open unless you possess the password. The password is "Grace," and it cannot be earned.

There will be no bargaining and no temporary passes; either you have accepted God's grace—or you haven't.

For years, I have heard good people proclaim that they will be deserving of heaven based on their works, and sadly, many Christians believe the same thing. It's unsettling to think that there are so many who never understand the basic tenet of grace.

If our goal is two, an easy equation is one plus one. If our goal is God's grace, then it requires humility through repentance plus faith in the person of Jesus Christ. Though it is true that humility in this equation is contained in faith, there is no faith without humility. It is possible to humble yourself before God and never believe in the resurrected Christ. Likewise, it is possible to believe in the resurrected Christ and never truly repent. One without the other will always equal one, and remember that two is our goal. If you do not do both, then you might as well do neither, because the goal will never be met. I do believe that there are differing degrees of hell, and if performing one task without the other helps keep you from future sins, then it would be in your best interest to do so, but it will never equal grace.

Humble yourself before God and repent. Believe in the fact that Jesus died for your sins and rose from the dead= God's free gift of eternal life also known as grace

D) Origins of Our Existence

"So God created man in his own image, in the image of God he created him; Male and female he created them. God blessed them and said to them, be fruitful and increase in number, fill the earth and subdue it. Rule over the fish of the sea and the birds of the air and over every living creature that walks on the ground."

Genesis 1:27–28

The Bible is the only book known to modern man that describes our origins in complete detail. The only books that come close are the "borrowed" or "altered" books that stem from the Bible. The Bible describes human nature, the nature of the cosmos, and the plan for both.

Our true nature is displayed in the first few chapters of the Bible. God created Adam and Eve in his own image and bestowed upon them free will—and it didn't take long for them to make unwise choices.

In the Bible, the nature of the universe is shown to be expanding and cooling, which coincides with modern physics. This model of the universe as we know it today is not available in any other ancient scriptures. The Bible taught it first.

People who deny the biblical explanation for our existence intrigue me. Throughout the years, I have heard multiple explanations for our origin. Obviously, evolution is the most common, but there have been others; aliens, multiple gods, and illusory existence come to mind. I have yet to hear a single explanation that remotely compares to the account given in Genesis. If we remove our rebellious nature and simply view the question from a standpoint of logic, we can see that all other accounts contain an agenda. Likewise, God has an agenda, but it is easily discerned from our own. If the explanation of our existence is to serve ourselves, then the man-made accounts of our origin will do just fine. However, if our purpose is to serve God, then we must submit to his revelation.

God describes our origin and nature to a T, and he leaves very little to doubt. We can try to rationalize other options, but they will require far greater leaps of faith than that of the biblical account.

E) Morality of Man

"Sin is an act performed by reasonable creatures. As creatures made in the image of God, we are free moral agents. Because we have a mind and a will, we are capable of moral action."

R. C. Sproul

"When tempted, no one should say, 'God is tempting me.' For God cannot be tempted by evil, nor does he tempt anyone; but each one is tempted when, by his own evil deeds, he is dragged away and enticed. Then after desire has conceived, it gives birth to sin; and sin, when it is full grown gives birth to death."

James 1:13–15

You've heard it said that we can't legislate morality. That would be true, unless we use the Bible as our compass. If all the legislators, lawyers, and judges used the Bible to decide right and wrong, then the world would be a safer and cleaner place. We know that it is wrong to kill; the Bible says it to be so. We know it is wrong to commit adultery; the Bible tells us that too. Pornography, idolatry, pride, and gluttony are considered to be wrong by most people, and the Bible tells us that we are right to think of them as such.

Whatever deed is considered wrong by the majority is explained in the Bible. True, there are many deeds that are no longer considered wrong by the majority, but that doesn't make those actions right. Sexual contact prior to marriage is considered acceptable behavior by most Americans, but that speaks more to the erosion of our overall morality than to anything else. Simply because refraining from an act seems unrealistic in our age doesn't give us autonomous immunity to perform it.

God gave us a moral compass. It is revealed in his Word and hardwired into our brains. This is evident when we feel guilt, and I would challenge you to find an immoral action that is not detailed in the Bible. When we realize that pride itself is at the core of most of our misdeeds, and that our rebellious nature caters to that pride, finding a wrong that God hasn't yet revealed as being wrong would be a hard find.

Pastor Rick Warren was recently asked if he would change his opinion of homosexuality being wrong if science proved there to be a genetic inclination for homosexuality. He simply stated, "No. I have a genetic inclination to have sex with every beautiful woman that walks by but I choose to refrain from doing so." Thanks, Rick. It's good to know that somebody else has that problem too. He could have added, "Who am I to decide what is right and wrong?" Having a genetic disposition in no way excuses our actions. I have a genetic inclination to be a touch edgy, but that won't excuse me from yelling at everybody who annoys me. Just because you believe that you are predisposed to be a certain way doesn't mean that you can't choose to do the opposite.

The Bible is the ultimate book of morality. Some will argue that the God of the Old Testament wasn't acting in an immoral way when he destroyed humanity with a flood. I would argue that if he did it again, he would be justified in doing so.

Following God's moral code is freedom from what oppresses us. We often think of morality as a hindrance, that ball and chain that holds us in bondage and keeps us from our true desires. Like many things in life, the opposite is true: sin is bondage and we are its servant.

F) Meaning of Life

"I know, O Lord, that a man's life is not his own: It is not for a man to direct his steps."

Jeremiah 10:23

"For a philosophy that defines life apart from God, there is a plethora of options, each necessarily forfeiting the right to judge anyone else's choice. For a philosophy that espouses God, life is directed by the concepts and precepts that are revealed by His character and purpose."

Ravi Zacherias

In blunt terms, our true meaning in life is that we were created to serve God and that is our primary purpose. There are other purposes like loving our neighbors and helping those in need, but they are superseded by our primary purpose. If we take this to the next level, we can conclude that without our primary purpose in hand, all others are rendered meaningless.

There are many wonderful events unfolding as your life passes by. Each filled with joy or pain. During these events, we can choose to direct our attention toward God or ourselves. When we choose to help others while neglecting God, we will be seen as a charitable person, but we will be unknown to God. To know the God is to love him, and it is hard to love somebody you have never met. If we fail to form a personal relationship with God, he'll simply say that he never knew us. As humans, we see the good works of people every day, and are inclined to believe that if there is a heaven, surely these people will have a place. Unfortunately, that is not what the Bible says. We need to put our priorities in proper order: knowing and loving God first and everything else second.

A good friend of mine rests on his morals. He has said on many an occasion that if there is a heaven, surely God would let him in, based on the type of life that he has led. I have informed him that the Bible doesn't spell it out in that manner. Amazingly, people get angry when you inform them of what was written thousands of years before. Apparently, there are some who think that Christians are responsible for the inner workings of salvation, but I can assure you that we are not. I would like to believe that being a good person on the human scale of what is considered good would punch your ticket to heaven, but I don't make the rules.

God made man in his image and we were meant to worship and adore him; that is the ultimate meaning of life. When we love and adore him, our lives are used in meaningful ways toward his plan. If, on the other hand, we omit God from our lives, we are left to serve our own plan, which ends in death. There are two paths to choose from—the well-beaten path of those serving their own purpose and the one that leads home to the Lord. Regardless of your achievements, when you are on the wrong road, your endeavors—both good and bad—will be in vain. If we make our way to the right road, we will be free to follow God in his plan, and have the assurance that while we will fall from time to time, God will be there to right the ship.

"The kingdom must not be understood as merely the salvation of certain individuals or even as the reign of God in the hearts of his people; It means nothing less than the reign of God over his entire created universe. The kingdom is not man's upward climb to perfection but God's breaking into human history to establish his reign and to advance his purpose."

Anthony Hoekema

G) Heaven

"There have been times when I think that we do not desire heaven, but more often, I find myself wondering whether, in our heart of hearts, we have ever desired anything else."

C. S. Lewis

There is no complete description of heaven in the Bible and I've yet to meet a person who has spent time in heaven and then returned with a report. We do know that it will be a place of eternal happiness and joy, and the words of the scriptures tell us that it will be a physical realm. We will be given new bodies and a new earth. Many people have the misconception that we will be floating in a spiritual realm, trying to earn wings. Just as Jesus was resurrected in the human form, believers will as well.

There is a lot left to the imagination when we think of heaven. I try to imagine a perfect world without our crushing pride. It would be a world without physical pain, emotional anguish, and more than anything else, a world without fear. If we see the beauty that life has to offer us in this temporal age and if we can, for a moment, shield our eyes from evil, then we have seen a glimpse of heaven.

Heaven will not be one long church service. True, we will have a defined purpose to worship Jesus, but we will do many other activities while focusing our attention towards him. As humans, we were made to work. If your job is to make music and sing, then you might be singing in heaven. If you work the land for harvest or you care for animals, then you might be doing those tasks in heaven. If you are a dentist, then you will be doing something entirely different, because tooth decay will fall by the wayside, along with all other decay. Whatever our duties may be, they will be done with complete joy. It is hard for us to envision a world without boredom and pain, but that doesn't mean that one doesn't exist.

Heaven will have:

Purpose
Eternal joy
Fellowship and good cheer
Endless activities

Heaven will not have:

Aimless wandering
Pain and suffering
Loneliness
Boredom

Heaven will be a place where you will be eternally fulfilled. Whatever you feel makes you happy in this life will pale in comparison to what heaven has to offer. There are people who actually believe that they would be better off in hell, because at least they won't be bored. It is true that hell probably isn't boring, but it will be completely devoid of God, and God equals all things good.

Anything that you can point to as being good, you will find a thousand-fold in heaven. If family and friends are good things, they will be enhanced in heaven. If boredom and solitude are seen as bad things, they will be abolished in the eternal kingdom. Basically, heaven will be paradise on a new earth. It will be a one world government with Jesus as president. It is waiting for us, and like a child who refuses to eat broccoli, many are doing everything possible to avoid it.

It is hard to say what we will be feeling when we first lay eyes on the Lord. The Christian band "Mercy Me." might have said it best when they sang, "I can only imagine." We are left to imagine, but it is our imagination that points us in the right direction. If we set our minds to eternity, our hearts will follow. Home truly is where the heart is!

"In my Father's house, there are many mansions; if it were not so, I would have told you: For I go to prepare a place for you."

John 14:2

If you can, imagine the perfect day, complete with the fellowship of all your favorite people. On this day, you learn at a rapid pace and help others with a completed form of love. You laugh and have good cheer, and your sense of pain and fear are not only in a state of void, they are forgotten altogether. Then, if you multiply that awesome feeling a thousand times over, then you have seen my personal view of what heaven will be like.

Just a Thought #15

Imagine that you spent forty years working in a coal mine. You might say it was a living hell. Then imagine the working conditions are a thousand times worse and you work around the clock. Then one day, you realize that you must spend another forty years in the mine ... times a thousand ... times eternity. Suddenly, the lights go out and still your turmoil continues. In hell, you would hope for conditions such as these!

Chapter 18

The Life of Jesus

The Incarnation, The Ministry, The Death, and Resurrection

Part 1: The Incarnation

"In the beginning was the Word, and the Word was with God, and the Word was God."

John 1:1

This is one of my favorite passages in the Bible. It goes back before the created time and describes two-thirds of the Trinity. When we replace "Word." with Jesus (since that is who it is pertaining to), the verse reads as follows:

In the beginning there was Jesus.

Even before time began, there was Jesus.

And Jesus was with God.

The Father and Son were together. This is two-thirds of the trinity.

And Jesus was God.

This equates Jesus as equal with God. Since we as Christians are taught that there is only one God, it can be therefore concluded that he is one person in at least two essences. When we add the Holy Spirit, we complete the Trinity.

Christmas is a magical time for many. Families gather across the country for celebration and give gifts to one another. The personal traditions vary, but the reason remains the same. It is a recognition that the Messiah of the Old Testament is born and will usher in a new covenant to all who believe. The miraculous way that Jesus became human is often scoffed at by secular America. They find the Virgin Birth beyond comprehension and therefore discard the whole idea. If God is able to create eyes that can see the earth from outer space and a brain that can calculate computer programs, then believing that the Virgin Birth as being anything more than child's play to God is ridiculous.

Our limitations are on display in all of our endeavors, but the simple fact that something appears impossible to us should in no way limit God. If we believe that God is just a larger version of ourselves and not omnipotent, then we are left to think of God's power as equal to ours. Basically, if you think that an event never occurred because it is not humanly possible, then maybe you should look beyond our limitations.

"Who, being in the very nature of God, did not consider equality with God something to be grasped. But made himself nothing, taking the very nature of a servant, being made in human likeness. And being found in appearance of a man, He humbled himself and became obedient to death."

Philippians 2:6–8

This is an amazing passage. Jesus is 100 percent God and 100 percent man at the same time. While human, he could not consider himself equal to God, so he humbled himself perfectly to the Father's will. The Father's will was that he become the sacrificial lamb and die on the cross and Jesus performed his Father's will perfectly for our salvation. This is not to be confused with an idea that Jesus is not equal to God. Jesus purposely relinquished his power to the Father's will to provide for his own purpose.

The incarnation is the beginning of the gospel. Without this humbling act of becoming human, the ministry, sacrifice, and resurrection could not have happened. It truly is a time for celebration and praise. This one prophecy performed by God has opened the door for all, and it will remain open until our time is done.

Next Christmas, when you give to your relations, take a moment to reflect on the reason for the season. It's more than a celebration of the birth of Jesus; it is a celebration of the promise brought to us in his person for everlasting life. Jesus is the way, the truth, and the life, and it all began on the first Christmas, some two thousand years ago.

Part 2: The Ministry

"This is why I speak to them in parables."

"Though seeing, they do not see: Though hearing they do not hear or understand."

Matthew 13:13

Jesus spoke in parables. He purposely did this so that those who have faith will understand his words and see the truth. For those without faith, the words will fall on deaf ears. This is as true today as it was two thousand years ago. When we come to the Lord, we see new things and we see old things in new ways.

The ministry of Jesus began when he was about thirty and lasted until his crucifixion three years later. During those years, Jesus had many followers; there were the twelve disciples, but also many others who were blessed to have faith and understand his teachings. Jesus performed miracles and healed and fed many. More than anything else, he spoke; he spoke of heaven and hell, he spoke of the coming kingdom and our need to repent, and he spoke about truth, morality, and salvation.

There are countless messages that Jesus conveyed to his listeners, and his words had a common theme: they were authoritative. Jesus never told anybody how he felt, he told them how it is. Nowhere else in the history of man has a historical character spoken in such terms. Jesus never worried about hurt feelings or being misunderstood simply because he left little to discuss. Trying to imagine a person who never rethinks his thoughts is mind-boggling. Jesus was quick to rebuke his followers, and never once said he was sorry for doing so. His nature was completely separate from our own, and although he felt pain, toiled in the sun just as we do, and he walked for miles and probably had blisters on the bottoms of his feet he acted only for the pure love for others; to which no other historical character can lay claim. What Jesus didn't have was a guilty conscience; he had no reason for one. He was a perfect man and wholly God at the same time.

Skeptics have spent the last two thousand years trying to equate Jesus with a good moral teacher, but it remains foolish to try. C. S. Lewis coined the phrase, "Lord, Liar, or Lunatic" and when we read the words of Jesus, we are left to these three choices. Jesus said that he was God on many occasions. If it is true, no real problem arises, but if Jesus is not God, then only two options remain. If he was lying, he would be much more than the typical liar like you and me; he would be the greatest deceiver of all time. Deception is the greatest attribute of evil and the devil himself. Therefore, if Jesus the *liar* is selling the idea of his divinity to the masses, he would be closer to bringing hell to the forefront than any type of heavenly kingdom. The last option left for the skeptic is that Jesus was insane. By all accounts, Jesus was not insane. The Jews who hated Jesus never said he was a lunatic; they called him a *heretic* and prompted his death, but his lucidity was never in question. In all ancient writings on the life of Jesus, not a single group of people—the Jews, the Romans, or the Greeks—ever laid claim to Jesus being anything but of sound mind.

The ministry of Jesus is vast and complex, and it is a lifelong study. I have touched on his basic theme and his manner of speech. But what was his message? The overall message is that he had come to usher in a new covenant, and that through him, we can have everlasting life. He spoke about how to live our lives and what is considered right and wrong, but more than anything, Jesus spoke about priorities. As flawed humans, our priorities are way out of whack; Jesus set the record straight.

"The fear of the Lord is the beginning of knowledge."

Proverbs 1:7

Without the fear of God, we are left out of the loop. We must submit to the Lord before we can expect to truly understand what he is telling us. Jesus knew that many who personally saw him would never understand his teachings, and that through the remaining centuries, the song would remain the same. Jesus declared his command to priorities in the book of Matthew

"But seek first his kingdom and his righteousness, and all these things will be given to you as well."

Matthew 6:33

All that is desirable is awaiting those who *seek first the kingdom of God and his righteousness.* Jesus didn't say that it would be a good idea to do so; he said that you are required to do so. Being a Christian is more than being a member of a really cool club. It is utterly impossible to understand if you lack the fear of God and if you refuse to seek his kingdom. All the great writers in the historical record had one thing in common: they all learned to read first. Likewise, faith must be obtained in a proper order, and to do otherwise would be as foolish as trying to scale Mount Everest in shorts and a tank top.

Part 3: The Death and Resurrection

Most people are in agreement, skeptics and believers alike that *something* happened two thousand years ago that changed the course of history. While Christians have spent the last two millennia rejoicing, the skeptics have been hard at work trying to explain the phenomenon. The death and resurrection of Jesus is a convicting event to a believer. Without this occurrence, Christianity would hold very little water, and the world would be in an even greater state of disarray. The greatest happening in the historical record is scoffed at by skeptics and ignored by even more. When challenged to explain away the death and resurrection, the skeptic has two choices:

1) Jesus wasn't really dead, or

2) Jesus never rose from the dead.

There is wide evidence from varying parties that Jesus was beaten, crucified, and placed in a tomb and that the body disappeared. The skeptic will concede that these events occurred, but will whitewash the events to deny the deity of Christ. They are left with completely implausible theories that show more of their own nature than that of a believer. The theories are widespread, and although they cannot compare with the biblical account, we should examine a few of the more popular ones:

1) Jesus wasn't dead; he was just close to death and healed completely in three days.

Answer:

First off, the Roman executors knew what they were doing. They were trained in the field of death and would never take a living man down from the cross. Secondly, Jesus had lost so much blood that even if he could have recovered and been able to walk, talk, and dine with more than five hundred people, it would have taken months. Three days alone in a cold tomb with nobody tending to your wounds is not going to make you well. Finally, they pierced his heart with a spear and it exploded. I think that would spell the end for most people who are a block away from a modern-day emergency room, let alone a carpenter on a cross at Calvary two thousand years ago.

2) Jesus never rose from the dead.

A) The Romans or the Jews stole the body.

Answer:

If the body was stolen by persons who were denying the divinity of Christ, they could have paraded the body throughout Jerusalem. If that had happened, I wouldn't be typing these words and I could get something to eat because I'm really hungry about now.

B) The disciples stole the body.

Answer:

First and foremost, they were in hiding and terribly afraid that they were next. The disciples were distraught over the fact that Jesus was dead, and possessed zero understanding as to why. Secondly, the tomb was guarded by Roman soldiers who would have faced crucifixion themselves if they were to fail in their duties. These soldiers were found in a state of confusion and had no idea how the body had disappeared, but would have loved to have laid blame on a mob of the eleven remaining disciples. Finally, they had no reason to steal the body; he was buried in a tomb of the rich. They had nowhere else to place him in mind, and they believed that all was lost and that they might have been wrong in stating his divinity.

The resurrection is an even greater mystery to the non-believer. They will concede that something happened that changed the nature of those who claimed to have seen Jesus in a physical body after the crucifixion and death, but have yet to offer a plausible explanation. Jesus appeared before the disciples and about five hundred others in his resurrected human body. He walked with them, he talked with them, and he even ate with them. He was a physical being. What stemmed from these appearances changed everything; the disciples went from fear of persecution to proclamation of Christ's divinity overnight. They were all eventually martyred for their belief in the risen Christ (with the possible exception of John, who may have avoided being martyred but never went silent on his belief). It truly takes an amazing event to change the very nature of men in such a swift manner. If you have ever questioned the death and resurrection of Jesus, ask yourself these questions: If the disciples were lying about the risen Christ, would they be willing to die for that lie? If Jesus never rose from the dead, would Christianity have spread faster than any other religion on the face of the earth? Have you ever tried to keep a secret with ten friends about a lie that you all were instituting? And finally, if you do not believe in the risen Christ, have you ever wondered what did happen to those early believers that made them perpetuate such a fabrication and be willing to die for it?

In the two thousand years that these questions pertaining to the resurrection have been bouncing around in the minds of the skeptics, they have come up with only a couple of laughable explanations. Keep in mind that there were at least 511 people who claimed to have seen the resurrected Jesus, and through these people, the Church of Christianity was born. These people were willing and ready to die for their claim, and many did. The fact that these people made their claims and that many died for their faith is not argued by skeptics, but the reason is still under scrutiny. Here are there two most common theories

1) Pride

Obviously these people were believers in Christ's divinity before the crucifixion and were not willing to admit that they were wrong. They had invested way too much in their faith and were unwilling turn back.

Answer:

The entire ministry lasted a mere three years, and most of the five hundred had never met Jesus prior to his post-death appearance or at the very least his entry into Jerusalem days before. I find it hard to believe that the people who gave their life for this investment of a short period of time would do so for a lie.

2) Mass Delusion

They wanted to believe so badly that they experienced a simultaneous illusion of the risen Christ. They were all insane to the point of death.

Answer:

The skeptics who believe this theory are the ones who should be checking their sanity. Nowhere in recorded history has a group of people gone insane at the same time and on such a massive scale. Even the Jim Jones fanatics who spent years being brainwashed, would have refrained from the Kool-Aid if they felt they had a choice. A large group of people simply do not go from a state of sanity to insanity overnight, especially with the exact same delusion.

That's it! Two thousand years of research and that is the best the skeptics have to offer to explain the death and resurrection of Jesus Christ? The bottom line is that it cannot be explained in any other rational terms other than the biblical account. This event not only paves a way toward a saving grace, it also convicts the believer. This single historical event elevates Jesus as much more than a prophet or a good moral teacher; he can be nothing less than Lord and Savior.

The death and resurrection of Jesus Christ is the essential occurrence that provides for our salvation. Though it is a mystery how it works, I believe that it does. Without this ultimate sacrifice, Christians are left without a reasonable belief system. It would be the equivalent of a baseball team trying to win the pennant prior to the invention of the ball. It is the essential belief that makes me a Christian, as it is the only event in human history that I could never get past. It truly convinced me to believe and trust in the Lord Jesus Christ.

I stated above that the resurrection was hard for me to get by and that rejecting it seemed impossible. People reject God every day and the true reason may surprise you. Ravi Zacharias put it best when he stated:

"A man rejects God neither because of intellectual demands nor because of the scarcity of evidence. A man rejects God of a moral resistance that refuses to admit his need for God."

Pride, pride, pride! It is the one constant that stands in the way of eternal salvation and is the main tool used by our enemy.

Chapter 19

How Wretched Art Thou

"Amazing Grace, how sweet the sound, that saved a wretch like me. I once was lost, but now am found, was blind, but now I see."

Part 1: Self-Examination

Self-examination is the jagged little pill that we all must swallow. As for myself, I could write volumes on my wicked ways. This might be surprising to some of you, based on my belief system that I have detailed in previous chapters, but make no mistake: I have problems. I would be lying to you if I said that my indiscretions haven't improved; they have, but not by my own means. God has greatly influenced my life and has partially freed me from my wayward path. I continue to fall, but every time I do, God helps me to my feet, and when I recognize him in doing so, my falls become fewer and fewer. In a poetic way, I will explain my current state of existence.

I am easily annoyed and short on patience. Day-to-day mannerisms of others who do not adhere to my standards instantly upset me. They are mostly trivial items; standing inches away from the selections at the video store while preventing others from seeing the selections is one. Accelerating on the right-hand side of a passing lane when previously traveling at the speed of smell is another. Telling your life story at the checkout stand is always a good way to make my blood boil. Basically, I have zero patience when it comes to common courtesy.

I need to show patience and reverence with other people. The Bible tells me so, and the Holy Spirit is guiding me to this end.

I sometimes hope for the failure of certain endeavors of others to help me process my own personal status in life. It saddens me to admit this, but it is true. When I hear of a friend's accomplishment, I often worry about my own shortcomings and secretly hope for the score to even in my favor.

My pride is a hard mountain to scale. Although I know that vast treasures await me in God's kingdom, and by any standard have obtained eternal riches, I still forget that the world is dying and that rat race is already won.

I sometimes treat my immediate family as strangers. I have been unkind to my family out of self-pity so many times that I lost count. I have said so many hurtful things, it is a wonder that they remain by my side. Making a mountain out of a molehill is sometimes my favorite pastime. My wife may have seven pairs of shoes displayed at different locations in the living room, and because of this I sometimes treat her like she were one of the 9/11 terrorists. When things don't go as planned, I will rehash all the previous failures in an attempt to explain "Why me?" When that doesn't help, and it never does, I have a tendency to blame those around me.

Treating loved ones badly and using self-pity to defend those actions is a real problem for me. I know that it is wrong, and through God's grace, I have come to grips with the issue and slowly, I am learning to put it behind me.

I have strong earthly desires that sometimes consume me. I daydream about worldly goods and sexual deviancy, and although I would never cheat on my wife, I fantasize on way too many occasions. I think about the glitter and gold that this world has to offer, and I covet them.

Every time my mind wanders onto one of these topics, the Holy Spirit redirects my thinking. I have fewer desires than I did yesterday, and hopefully this condition will improve with God's will.

I sometimes hate the sinner. There are times when I'll see a homosexual walking down the street and I'll loathe everything about them. Sometimes, I'll watch an episode of *Cops* and I'll show zero compassion for the criminals being arrested. I've seen videos of people being beheaded in the Middle East, and I want instant vengeance and often replace righteous anger with flat-out hatred.

I know that vengeance is the Lord's, but I have hateful feelings that are sometimes hard to decompress. When I see the grace that God has bestowed on me, it should be easy to pass it along, but sometimes I forget. Through prayer, I have slowly improved in this area. I need to be reminded of my own personal problems to keep my hatred at bay, and God reminds me of this every day.

To summarize, I am a cranky, impatient person who is easily annoyed. I am pride-filled and hope for justification from my peers. I have deep desires for possessions that I will never be able to keep and I have a tendency to hate perversion and I would, on occasion, like to hurt the people responsible.

Can you believe that I am almost always described as a good guy? Seeing yourself for who you really are is tough to do, but in realizing that everybody is in the same boat at the point of accepting grace can help ease the pain. I can say with complete certainty that God is correcting my problems. It can be a slow and painful process, but it gets better every day. Knowledge of the fact that I am helpless in my recovery puts me in the back seat, and when hoping for a change in our own nature, *that* is the best place to be. People do change, but it requires much more than help from above; it requires stewardship from above.

Part 2: My Current Condition

My current condition is bad and will remain so until I die. At that point, the Lord will finish his handiwork and complete me and make me righteous. This by no measure means that he will not continue to improve my situation in this life, but I will be an unfinished project until the next level, which comes after death. My previous condition prior to coming to the Lord was far worse as I had all my current problems and a plethora of others. I can honestly say that God has freed me from many bad habits of my previous self. Amazingly, even back in the days of old, I was considered a "good guy" by most people. I guess when you look at my life and compare it to the purely evildoers, it can look pleasing—but when compared to God, it has the ultimate light shining on it, and in this light, we can see how far I had actually fallen.

I am indeed a wretched soul, but I am less wretched than I was yesterday and God willing, I'll be better tomorrow. We cannot measure a heart by its current condition; it must be measured from its previous condition and God's plan for its future purpose.

Chapter 20

Addiction

Part 1: We Are All Addicts

If a person is described as having an addictive personality, it usually takes the form of a negatively perceived vice: drugs, alcohol, pornography, etc. I stated before that I believe we all serve some form of god, and in that servitude, we find our addiction. Every human being on the face of the earth is an addict, and it is more than a learned behavior or an inheritance; it is our nature. A good person can be addicted to work and lose track of his family, while another might be addicted to spending time with his family and lose his job. We can adapt and prioritize our time to help solve these problems, but our addiction will rise again in other areas. Whatever floats your boat, even if your compulsion is to be the most well rounded individual alive, you are still addicted to that compulsion. It cannot be escaped, you cannot outrun it; whether healthy or destructive, it remains in our very being. So if we are all addicts and it is in our nature to be so, then why is it in our nature? Simply stated, we were made to be addicted to love, and we fill that void with anything that soothes our addiction and eases the pain.

Part 2: The Good Addict

For some, our addiction is very apparent and self-destructive. An alcoholic or a drug user can be easily spotted by appearance and in the wake of the turmoil following them, but what about the person who appears in control of his life in every way? If we can imagine a person who works diligently at a worthwhile job and loves his family, friends, and neighbors with all his heart while avoiding corrupt vices, then surely, he must not be an addict. I would argue that he is addicted to the good life. The world is filled with addictions that appear to be quality virtues (and in many cases, they are), but that doesn't mean that they won't eventually lead to destruction. If it is true that heaven cannot be earned, then having the finest of virtues and holding true to them for an entire lifetime will still land you on the bankruptcy spot on the wheel of fortune.

Recently, I heard Rush Limbaugh explain to a caller why certain politicians lie to save their positions, when it would appear to all others that they are digging their own political grave. Limbaugh (who knows a thing or two about addiction after his battle with pain pills) simply stated, "Politicians are addicted to power and when a person has an intense addiction, they will do whatever is needed to feed that addiction." The caller then voiced in confusion, "Even if they know it will lead to their own dismay?" Limbaugh answered, "Yes, because all addiction leads to self-destruction and the addict knows that it is inevitable." Rush is right to assume that addiction leads to destruction, even if you're merely addicted to life and its beauty.

Part 3: The Right Addiction

We all have a primary addiction that stands above the others. This is the addiction that cannot be left alone for long and will eventually consume us. For a Christian, it is our addiction to God's love and our reciprocation of that love. It should be apparent that we all have a deep-rooted desire to love and be loved. God gave us that desire and our addictive nature as well. The problem comes to light when we try to fill our addiction with anything apart from its original intention. When we put God first and focus on him all other addictions, while many will remain, will become trivial and easily rendered as irrelevant.

Robert Palmer might have been on to something when he said that we might as well face it we're addicted to love.

"Love the Lord your God with all your heart, soul, and mind. This is the greatest commandments. The second most important is similar: Love your neighbor as much as you love yourself."

Jesus in Matthew 22:37-39

Jesus said that we are to love God with all our heart, soul, and mind, and that this is the greatest of the commandments. If an architect loves his work with all his heart, soul, and mind, then he will probably be a good architect. He will also be addicted to architectural study, literature, and design. I find it interesting that Jesus uses the word *all* when describing our command for loving God. He doesn't imply that we save *some* of our love for him or that we share our love equally with him and others; he wants *all* our love. If this is true, then what love will remain to fulfill the second commandment to love our neighbors as ourselves? When you have your priorities in order and you truly love God in the way that is commanded, then you will not love another human being or anything else worldly in the same manner that could otherwise be possible. You can love anything you choose with all your heart, soul, and mind, but if you choose to love God in this commanded way, then all other love you give will be true love stemming from God himself and not yourself. We can love God and share his love with others, but we cannot love the world and share in God's love at the same time.

Humans will remain flawed, and our addictions will always be there to annoy even the most just among us. When we put God first, we will soon realize that we are free to move away from the countless destructive addictions, because we will have found the only true and just addiction that leads to eternal life.

Chapter 21

What to Do?

Part 1: Finding Faith

Now that you have seen a glimpse of what is considered Christian thought, what should you do with this information? If you find it distasteful and beyond belief, then I guess you should carry on as before. If, on the other hand, you have found this book intriguing and you want to experience God's grace, then you can start with these simple steps.

1) Look at the stars in the sky and take time to admire the quiet streams and vast oceans. Carefully examine the animal kingdom and plant life that can be seen at every turn. God has told us that the creation itself is enough evidence to believe in him and that all will be without excuse.

2) After you have come to a logical conclusion that there must be a God, realize that he gave you a conscience for a reason. It is pertinent that you fear God, because that is the beginning of knowledge. You must come to grips with the fact that you will be held accountable for your actions.

3) Now that you have a belief in a Creator and you realize that he is to be feared, you must now seek out a place in his kingdom. He promises you that if you seek him, you will find him.

4) Okay, if you now believe that you know who God is, how do you receive his free gift of grace?

The following information is not my own. It is derived from the most common tenants found in the writings of Christian theologians throughout history. Far be it from me to tell any individual how to obtain salvation; I can only relay the message as I understand it from those who I deem as reliable sources. Therefore, it will remain in your best interest to seek the heartfelt advice from a trusted family member or a professional before taking the following steps.

a) Believe with all your heart and soul that Jesus Christ is your Lord and your God.
b) Humble yourself before him and admit your sins.
c) Repent and pray for his forgiveness, and he will answer that prayer.
d) Openly receive his gift of saving grace and the Holy Spirit will redirect your life.

If you are not convinced by this simple book, where should you look for more information on the subject?

I would submit that any questions about life can be answered in the Bible. I realize that it can be difficult for many to understand without your pastor's help. Maybe that is why we have churches. Praying to understand will help in more ways than one, but if you feel that you need a book or two to read prior to reading the ultimate book of life, I can make a few suggestions:

The Case for Faith by Lee Strobel is a good place to start. Strobel was a skeptic who took his examination on the road and asked many questions directed at scholars of theology that are not of the softball manner. Overall, it is an easy read and should perk the curiosity of even the most hardened of skeptic. Strobel has many other books in the Case for... series. *The Case for Christ* is an examination of the life of Jesus and is written in the same format. *The Case for Creation* is also a good read, especially for the skeptic using science to deny God.

Mere Christianity by C. S. Lewis is an amazing book that describes in detail what it means to be a Christian. It starts with the nature of man and ends with the very nature of God and his purpose. This book is not an easy read, as Lewis writes with an Old English style that is distinctly his own. The information contained in any of his many books is incredible, but it takes time to and patience to understand. *The Screwtape Letters* is a challenging book wherein Lewis takes the side of a demon named Screwtape. This is the most cleverly written book that I've ever read and one of the more insightful. Whatever you do, avoid this book until you have a general understanding of theology or you might never open the subject again.

Any book by Ravi Zacharias, Josh McDowell, or R. C. Sproul would be recommended to inspire a seeker. There are countless books written for the sole purpose of directing the seeker in the right direction. The aforementioned authors are some of my personal favorites, but you will find your own favorites who best speak to you.

Once again, I would suggest reading *The Case for Faith* and see where that leads you.

Once you have accepted the gift of grace, the Bible will become your personal handbook for life. It contains everything that you need to know and everything you could possibly desire. It is complete and without error and should be held in the hands of those who take it as such. The Bible can and will answer all the bigger questions while remaining true to the *will of God and his purpose.*

Part #2: The Fourth Quarter

Being raised in the American culture, I have been entrenched in the professional sporting world. There are certain clichés that are used by reporters and commentators that depict the state of performance of any particular team during the season. If a playoff-bound team is suffering through a losing streak toward the end of the regular season, we will often hear commentators wonder if they will be able to flip a switch and play at their proven ability once the playoffs commence. If you are so inclined to place matters of faith in neutral while waiting for a particular moment to devote your attention to God, then keep this in mind: when you left the age of accountability, you entered the playoffs; there are three minutes remaining in the fourth quarter of game seven. You're down by ten points and your teammate Kobe just fouled out. Eventually, the buzzer will sound and therefore, flipping the switch now might be in your best interest. Time goes by quickly, and you will never know when the last musical chair of eternal life will be filled. It's probably a good idea to find a seat in the kingdom sooner rather than later.

This little book was not intended to convince you of anything more than the fact that you should be curious and seek God, and that apathy and laziness in doing so will lead to destruction. I hope that I have accomplished my goal and that you will leave this book to another and move on from here with a yearning to know more. Remember that this is a layman's guide, and should be taken as such. There are people in every community across our Nation who, through years of study, have obtained a far better understanding than I. Be ready and willing to seek their help with any concern you may have.

May God bless you in your search!

Chapter 22

Some final thoughts

Part 1: My Two Fathers

I have two fathers: my paternal father and my eternal Father, and someday I will be with both. For many years, I doubted my dad's salvation. I mentioned earlier that he was not a church-going kind of guy. In fact, he was anything but. He was a good man in many areas, but he kept whatever beliefs he held to himself. He drank a lot of beer and smoked about fifty cigarettes a day. There were times when he would say the most hurtful things and remain silent in a response to sorrow. My dad had been baptized several years before his death, mostly out of fear, but he never really showed much change in his behavior. On the plus side, he was the most generous, hard-working, and caring person I have ever met and he was my hero. There are few words that he left me with, but the ones that he did are precious to me now, and are extremely helpful in my everyday life.

My dad passed away in 2002. He had battled prostate cancer years before, and when it returned, it consumed his entire body. A few days before he entered into a coma, I stopped by to see him. He was heading to bed, and I hollered down the hall that I loved him and he quickly responded with "I love you too, buddy." That was our final conversation. The next day, he suffered a stroke and was no longer able to communicate, but obviously somebody loved him even more than me. The first night after suffering the stroke, he sat up in bed and with complete clarity and asked my mom to pray with him. This was a shock to my mom for two reasons: first, he shouldn't be able to talk at all, and second, he had never prayed aloud in his life. My dad, at the age of seventy-two, literally on his deathbed, recited the Lord's Prayer and asked for forgiveness. He then rolled over and peacefully went to sleep. Three days later, he was gone, but he saved his final words for God. It was as if Jesus knew that my dad had made it halfway and wanted him to have a final chance at redemption, so he permitted him a moment of clarity in which to do so. My dad was truly blessed, but will we all be given that final chance? I know that my dad is in heaven, and the peace that comes with knowing this is a great gift to have.

My eternal Father is the great giver of grace. He has awarded me comfort in trying times and righted my ship so many times that I've lost count. He has promised me a kingdom that I could never lose, and when his will is done, I will realize it in all its grandeur. I could never explain the reasoning behind God granting my Dad a second chance for salvation, but I can say this: he most mercifully did!

Part 2: Contrasting Voices

I wanted to end this book with a beautifully written Christian poem, but copy write issues have hindered that idea and steered me towards an examination of poetry from differing worldviews. When I began reading the multitudes of poems that are currently at my fingertips, I began to wonder about poetry from the darker side of the aisle. I typed in "secular poetry" and had little success in my search, so I then typed in "atheistic poetry" and was taken into a frightening world of hatred that could only be portrayed in the worst of all horror films. I probably read about a hundred of these poems until I started to feel horns popping out of my forehead and realized that I had better turn the page.

The writers of these poems had some interesting pen names:

I-would-crucify-him-again
Devilish-gerl23
Vehement-rancor

I could actually visualize these characters sitting in dark rooms listening to AC/DC while writing their words of hate. After reading the first ten or so, it was very apparent that these atheistic poets were much more interested in bashing Christianity than describing anything of worth contained in their worldview. Poem after poem was littered with a sheer hatred for God. Not a single one spoke of the joy that could be found in an atheistic view. They truly are petitioning the most angry and hateful to join their ranks, because any human soul that has a remaining glimmer of hope left in them would run and hide at the first glance of these words.

This will sum up their writing style: hatred mixed with ridicule mixed with more hatred and a splash of darkness and then repeated until they run out of ink.

When reading over several Christian poems, I found a completely different attitude, devoid of hate and filled with hope and joy. The poems depicted on these Christian sites contained a message. They were purposeful and powerful and they avoided pointing fingers or looking down on other views. If it is true that a poem is a window into the poets heart then it can be noted that the atheist has a heart that is troubled to say the least, where as the Christian poet has at least foregone the hatred that will blind their ambitions and litter their work.

Final Thought

If God is all that is good and what goodness contained in each individual or a society is merely on loan from God, then what are we left with when we neglect God and basically ask him to leave? What will remain are memories of good, quality attributes that are fading as generations pass by. Love, compassion, and honesty will erode from our memory banks and be replaced with hate, indifference, and corruption. This conversion happens at a rate slow enough for many not to notice, but it picks up steam as the movement away from God increases. If God equals all that is good (and he does), then the absence of God (by any rule of deduction) can only equal bad. Emmanuel Kant once said that we cannot know God, but we had better pretend as if we can, because he knew the dire implications of denying the very idea of a deity. Even a hardened skeptic feared the idea of a wholly secular society and the chaos that would ensue. The world will remain a dangerous place and we will never evolve into a peaceful people until the return of Christ; therefore, we have a choice to make in our mindset. Which choice will we make as a society?

"Onward, Christian soldiers, marching on to war,
with the cross of Jesus going on before."

or

"Onward secular soldier, marching on to war,
with the state's mighty emblem, going on before."

End Notes

The Holy Bible by God
Mere Christianity by C. S. Lewis
Can Man Live Without God? by Ravi Zacharias
Jesus Among Other Gods by Ravi Zacharias
The New Evidence by Josh McDowell
Beyond Belief to Conviction by Josh McDowell
The Case for Faith by Lee Strobel
The Case for Christ by Lee Strobel
Heaven by Randy Alcorn
The Creator and the Cosmos by Dr. Hugh Ross
Essential Truths of the Christian Faith by R. C. Sproul
A Quest for Answers (The da Vinci Code) by Josh McDowell
Every Prophecy of the Bible by John F. Walvoord
The Purpose-driven Life by Rick Warren
The Dictionary of Philosophy and Religion by William L. Reese
Revelation Unveiled by Tim Lahaye
Radical Son by David Horowitz
2,000 Years of Disbelief by James A. Haught
Godless by Ann Coulter
Common Sense by Thomas Paine

Handbook of Today's Religions by Josh McDowell and Don Stewart
The Life of Jesus by Jon Courson
Christian Denominations by Ron Rhodes
The Next World War by Grant R. Jeffrey
The Lord of the Rings by J.R.R. Tolkien
Lonesome Dove by Larry McMurtry
The da Vinci Code by Dan Brown
The Secret by Rhonda Byrne

Additional Resources

Willingheart Ministries in Eagle Point, Oregon
Pastor and Teacher Rick Booye

Trail.org
LDS.com
Islam.com
Watchtower.org
Scientology.org
Religioustolerance.org
Buddhaweb.org
Hinduismtoday.com
Sacredtexts.com

Biblesoft: PC Study Bible Version 5
Containing the writings of Luther, Aquinas, Calvin, and a plethora of others

LaVergne, TN USA
26 October 2009
161905LV00003B/10/P